Businesses For Sale

How To Buy Or Sell
A Small Business

A Guide for Business Buyers,
Business Owners & Business Brokers

Peter Siegel, MBA

Peter Siegel, MBA
Businesses For Sale

Printed in the United States of America

ISBN: 0-9761985-2-5

Library Of Congress Control Number: 2004117784

Bulk Quantity Discounts:
This book and companion books from this publisher are available at quantity discounts for bulk purchases for educational, business or sales promotional use. For information regarding bulk purchases please call (800) 207-7478.

Publisher:
USA BizMart / www.USABizMart.com
9110-B Alcosta Blvd., #238
San Ramon, CA. 94583
(800) 207-7478

Other books by Peter Siegel, MBA, available from this publisher:
Selling a California Business -
      The Ultimate Guide for California Business Sellers!
Buying a California Business -
      The Ultimate Guide for Savvy Business Buyers!

See our website at: www.USABizMart.com

ACKNOWLEDGEMENT

For the past 15 years, it has been my privilege to be associated with a number of creative, dedicated and talented people in my work as a business buyer, business seller, business broker and founder and president of a growing organization that facilitates the marketing of small businesses for sale.

I am indebted to a number of professionals, too numerous to mention, from whom I have gained the education and the inspiration, as well as the ideas and the insights which I endeavor to share with others on the pages of this book.

I am grateful for the opportunities I have had to learn and to grow in this fascinating and vital area of business.

Peter Siegel, MBA
January, 2005

The one million plus new business owners every year in the U.S. are a little recognized part of our economy, but an important part. This book is dedicated to them, and those who will join their ranks in the future. It is the qualities these people exhibit which are responsible for the building of our country and our economy.

INTRODUCTION

Last year more than one million Americans – many of them unemployed or under-employed – took the matter of their economic well being into their own hands and began generating an income with their work in a vital but little recognized segment of our economy.

They bought small businesses, paying prices ranging from a few hundred dollars – perhaps even less – up to $1 million. The sellers of these small businesses were individuals and companies, including a number of franchisors.

The contribution these small business owners make to our economy doesn't get the attention of government officials or business writers, yet they constitute an important part of our economy, providing millions of jobs, paying hundreds of millions of dollars in taxes, and providing vital products and services in all 50 states.

Some of these business people will expand their little organizations into larger enterprises, becoming wealthy in the process. Some will fail. Most will work hard in their companies to provide for their families and to build something which they can sell when it comes time for them to retire, or go on to a larger business.

At a time when mega-corporations dominate the news, and sometimes our lives, we might neglect to think about the owner of the corner grocery store, the woman who operates the dry cleaner we frequent, or the couple behind the counter at our favorite pizza take-out place. And yet these Americans, with their daily labor, the business dreams they cherish, and the entrepreneurial spirit that keeps them going, serve as a daily example of the qualities that built our country.

To these hard working and adventuresome business people, and to anyone who wants to join their ranks, this book is dedicated, with the hope that you will find in the pages that follow some ideas to assist you in successfully buying and selling your small business.

CHAPTER ONE

WHAT IT TAKES

An ancient parable relates the story of the man who was attracted by the legend of the *magnificent fish* to a beautiful lake in the middle of the woods, where he dropped his fishing line and waited for the catch of his life. He was filled with excited anticipation of the thrill he knew was soon to come. And he waited.

Others passed by, their fishing rods and bait in hand, on their way along the path to narrow creeks and lesser lakes on the outskirts of the woods. The man saw them every morning, and also every evening when they returned with their catch of moderate-sized fish with ordinary markings.

The man smiled to himself, for he knew he soon would put their meager results to shame when he hooked and landed the *magnificent fish*. And so he waited.

He waited in the days and weeks that passed, and he became hungry. He watched the others whose daily trek brought them sustenance but not the glory that would be his when he landed the *magnificent fish*. And as he waited and he watched the others with the product of their day's work, the man grew more resolute; more determined. He also became weaker and increasingly malnourished.

The man may be there still today, waiting, more resolute and more emaciated than ever.

A modern version of this tale might involve the owner of a small business (which I define as a company with a value of $1 million or less), who wants to retire and is waiting for the perfect buyer – someone with pockets full of cash who readily agrees to the seller's price and terms, even though logic and good business sense would argue that the business is substantially overpriced. Another modern parallel with the ancient fisherman is the buyer for a small business who waits expectantly for a highly profitable, fun and risk-free offering to come along at a very low price with easy seller financing.

Like the character in the parable, these 21st Century business people have a long wait ahead. And their decision to hold out for the magnificent deal, rather than to deal in reality is a choice made by a surprising number of buyers and sellers. In fact, it's the number one reason that more than half of would be sellers and buyers of small businesses, throughout the United States, are not successful in their efforts.

That's right: Fewer than half of the small businesses offered on the market – whether they are retail stores, restaurants, distribution companies, manufacturing enterprises or service firms – are ever sold. They simply close down or are taken over, at no (or nominal) cost, by a family member or business associate. And fewer than half of those who set out to purchase their own company are successful in their quest.

Despite these figures, my experience over the years as a business buyer, a seller and a business broker leads me to believe that for most every business there is a suitable buyer, and visa versa. What's wrong? Why do more than half fail on both the buy side and among sellers?

The unwillingness of sellers to accept market realities and to offer their businesses in a way that is consistent with those realities is a major reason why most of their businesses never are matched with a buyer. And a similar "reality blindness" on the part of buyers means that most won't realize the dream of owning their own businesses unless they select the riskier option of starting a company from scratch.

Are Americans so confused by the get-rich-quick stories in the media that they don't know how to adjust their sights to reality? Perhaps the biggest reason that many people are in "denial" about business reality, is fear: The fear of getting duped.

I get an awful feeling when it occurs to me I may have sold one or more of my businesses too cheaply. Or perhaps I paid too much for one of the companies I bought. No one wants to be a fool or a sucker. And that, perhaps is the major reason that we come to the marketplace with the attitude that we won't be "talked into" abandoning our ideas about business value even if those ideas keep us from moving forward toward our objectives. It was the same with the fisherman in the fable – he refused to throw his line into more fruitful waters for fear that he'd miss the chance at the *magnificent fish*.

Whether we are fearful, unduly influenced by overexposure to the hype emanating from TV and the movies, or simply lacking in solid knowledge, many of us are not in touch with the reality of the marketplace for small businesses, either as sellers or in the role of buyers.

Realistic About the Marketplace

And so, a key characteristic common to those who are successful buyers and sellers of small businesses, is the willingness to tune in to the realities of the market, and then to be guided by these realities when setting and meeting objectives.

For Seller's benefit

As a business owner planning to sell, you'll do well to learn what buyers are willing to pay for businesses in your area. It will take a bit of research, and you'll have to do the math in order to apply the prevailing formulae to your particular offering. The way to approach this problem will be treated in some detail in a chapter on business valuation, later in this book.

What sellers need to understand is that your business will be compared with others on the market. In order for what you are selling to be interesting to buyers, it should compare favorably with the competitive offerings when it comes to the asking price. Yes, yours may be the only retailer of toddler clothing and supplies in your neighborhood for sale at the time, but most prospective buyers are not focused on your kind of business. They want a certain income in relation to the investment they make in a small business. For many buyers, the small business could just as readily be a quick print franchise, a convenience store, a fast food franchise, or a profitable delivery service. There are many other options besides your offering. And the price and terms are critical factors in the desirability of a small business.

And this idea applies to the cash down payment required. You're not likely to get an all cash deal, at a fair price, because such a proposal would likely lose out to other offerings on the market that can be purchased with a down payment (of one-third or one-half the asking price), with the balance financed by the seller at reasonable pay-off terms. Those terms not only attract buyers' attention, they also shape the expectations of participants in the market.

Like every free market, the mechanism by which small businesses are offered for sale and then are purchased, is a complex and vibrant setting for the interaction of demand and supply. The genius of this system is that equilibrium is established, over time, between the demand and supply forces, which sets the prices and terms buyers are willing to pay, and sellers are willing to accept, for small businesses.

Naturally, there are a number of factors which influence the balance of supply and demand forces – factors such as type of business, characteristics of the marketplace and particulars of the business being offered. So there is no handy rule of thumb that applies in all cases.

But it's in the seller's best interests to get quickly educated about the real market, and to shape an offering accordingly. For an owner to place a small business up for sale without acknowledging and reflecting market realities can do more harm than good. The result may be not only the waste of the seller's time and resources, but also the stigma that comes about from fruitless exposure. Prospective buyers who might at one time have considered the business of possible interest – if only the price and terms were more reasonable – will come to regard the offering as undesirable, as it lingers on the market unsold. And that "bad rap" will cling to the business even if price and terms are later adjusted to coincide with the demands of the marketplace.

Among the most essential of those demands, incidentally, is that a business has a record of producing enough profits to justify its asking price. And a simple way to analyze this is to determine if the new owner will be able to take enough out of the business, through salary, profits, and so forth, to retire the debt to the seller, and/or other creditors, over a three to seven-year period, and also to be able to take home the money needed to live. The more readily the deal structure of price and terms can accommodate that requirement, the more likely the business will be sold in a reasonable period of time (six months or shorter).

And the Buyer's perspective

Imagine a business owner being able to build and manage a successful enterprise, or taking over a going concern and then beefing up its sales and profits, while navigating the unpredictable and challenging business environment in the U.S. Will this clever and resourceful entrepreneur suddenly lose his or her bearings and offer the business at a substantial discount? Not likely. And yet, isn't that what you, the buyer, are looking for – a healthy and profitable company offered at a below-market price?

Buyers hoping for an absolutely perfect business offering are at a disadvantage. They don't know when a good opportunity comes along and so they continue to wait, while less idealistic buyers are actively bidding on and purchasing companies which can meet their more realistic expectations.

As with unrealistic sellers, those buyers who'd rather harbor their wishes than deal with the facts of the marketplace may be able benefit from a little education so they're more knowledgeable about what is realistic to expect in the way of offerings.

A business broker I know carefully qualifies potential buyers to weed out those with unrealistic expectations. He maintains it's not a good use of his time to try working with people he does not think can be pleased. And he has a rather dramatic way of discharging those he won't work with and letting them know why. He hands them a lottery ticket and let's them know they have as good a chance to win the state-wide gambling game as to find the business that meets the needs they specified. Only a few of them get the point and agree to open up their requirements.

Importance of Patience

Having a firm grasp on the reality of the marketplace, however, does not compel a buyer or seller to take action at the first appearance of an opportunity. To participate effectively in the market for small businesses requires that your sense of what's possible and desirable, be tempered with the discipline to wait for the match that truly meets the objectives.

For the seller, it means patience as you sort through buyer candidates who may not be qualified in every important respect. It's great when a prospective buyer shows a strong interest in your offering. But that interest is meaningless if the buyer doesn't have the capacity – either the financial standing or the background of experience – needed to meet your requirements. In their eagerness to strike a deal, sellers sometimes are tempted to bend their rules about getting all the needed information to verify a buyer's qualifications at the outset of discussions. That's a mistake, potentially a costly one, if you engage in protracted negotiations and even find yourself focused on working out a deal with someone who, in the final analysis, should not have been considered a serious buyer candidate in the first place.

I've seen too many situations in which a seller was sweet-talked by an unqualified buyer who was generous with compliments and promises, but unable to perform when it came time for the moment of truth. A strategy practiced by some unqualified buyers is designed to take up the seller's time and, if possible, get the business off the market long enough to discourage other, more suitable purchaser candidates. Then with the trickster the only active prospective buyer, the seller may feel there is no choice but to go along with whatever meager cash and terms can be obtained from the sole active buyer.

The smart seller can avoid getting caught in this scam by refusing to deal with anyone who can't produce a financial statement demonstrating the financial ability to do the deal the way the seller has specified. It doesn't commit the buyer to meet your price and terms. It just means that they are capable, if they choose to do so. I know of circumstances in which sellers – or perhaps it was their brokers or agents – would not agree to an introduction for a prospective buyer until the buyer provided a letter from a banker affirming the buyer's stated financial capabilities.

And for the buyer of a small business, the quality of patience will help protect you from jumping into a transaction for an enterprise with a great deal of initial appeal, but major problems that make it a less than desirable purchase candidate. A supplier of "kit" cars who claimed a customer list filled with music, movie and sports celebrities, was able to convince buyers they should make an acceptable purchase offer, complete with a deposit check covering a substantial portion of the purchase price, before he would reveal details about the business. He went through this process, including a session of due diligence, with four different buyers, each of whom discovered the business records did not support the owner's revenue and profit claims. It's fortunate that none of the prospective buyers became committed to the deal before learning the truth. It probably was the seller's hope that someone could be tricked into removing contingencies and forced into buying the business at the advertised price – a price that was way too high, considering the company's actual performance.

Most deals for a small business include the well-established procedure which keeps the focus on the due diligence process. First the prospective buyer makes an offer with contingencies, then removes them and commits to the purchase only if and when satisfied that the performance of the business matches the statements and representations that were made about it. That procedure works quite well as long as the purchaser exercises patience throughout the stages of negotiations and then the due diligence analysis. It should be noted that for a business buyer to be successful, he or she must be willing to act decisively when the time comes. But it also is necessary that the buyer is willing to work patiently with the procedures which provide protection from getting rushed into a bad deal.

In many cases, it can take six months of promoting a small business for sale before the owner gets a satisfactory deal with a qualified buyer. And for buyers, the search can take a year, or more, before the desired objective is achieved – a suitable business is located, checked out and successfully purchased. With these time requirements, it's clear that when dealing with a small business, your patience is a virtue.

Conclusion

Among the most important qualities of a buyer or a seller of a small business is a firm grip on reality, including the recognition that the process takes time, and the ability to be patient so as not to rush into a bad deal.

KEY POINTS FROM THIS CHAPTER

❖ *A surprising number of buyers and sellers of small businesses are determined to hold out for the perfect deal, which is why more than half of the businesses offered for sale are never sold, and why so many would-be buyers are never successful at making a purchase.*

❖ *Despite these statistics, I believe there is a buyer for most every small business. But there also is an unwillingness of many sellers, as well as many buyers, to accept and deal with the real world of business sales. And I think that accounts for the high instance of their failure.*

❖ *A key factor in the unwillingness of would-be buyers and sellers to accept the facts of the marketplace in which they are involved, is the fear that they will err by entering into a deal that is inferior to what they could have achieved had they waited for the perfect buyer, or the perfect opportunity to come along.*

❖ *Owners wanting to sell their small businesses need to become informed about what is selling and for how much, so they can present their offerings accordingly. If a business does not make sense because the return on investment is too small, it is unlikely to sell.*

❖ *Not only the price but also the terms of an offering need to be appealing in order to make a business desirable to purchasers. A requirement that all cash be paid for a business means it will not compare favorably with competitive opportunities in which the seller will finance. More stringent terms make a company harder to sell.*

❖ *The genius of the free market for businesses offered up for sale is in the way the interaction of supply and demand leads to a balance around the proper price point for each company for sale – the price that buyers are willing to pay and sellers will accept.*

❖ *A number of other, more subtle factors play a role in adjusting a price for a business. They include type of business, characteristics of the market in which the business functions and the particulars of the business being offered.*

❖ *The seller who does not accurately reflect market realities when offering his or her business for sale, may be doing more harm than good to the marketing effort. Overpriced offerings, for example, can take on a stigma as unappealing businesses that will not be able to generate buyer interest even after the price is adjusted to more accurately accommodate the demands of the marketplace.*

❖ *An example of a marketplace demand is that a business generate enough earnings, in the form of profits, owner's salary and other owner benefits, to support the cost of the debt acquired to buy the business, and to provide a reasonable income for the buyer.*

❖ *Buyers should be aware that a person smart enough to build a successful business will not suddenly lose those smarts and offer a business with an exceedingly low price and particularly easy terms.*

❖ *To be successful at purchasing a business, buyers need to familiarize themselves with the realities of the marketplace and not set their sights, unrealistically, on finding the absolutely perfect business.*

❖ *One business broker gives lottery tickets to unrealistic buyers and tells them they are better off hoping for a lottery win because it takes less work and is just as likely to bring success as their finding and buying the perfect business.*

❖ *A seller may be so tempted to deal with a charming and interested buyer prospect that the important qualifying process is not strictly observed. That's a mistake. Sellers should be patient in the review of possible buyers and make sure that anyone who gets information about the business has demonstrated the ability to purchase it.*

❖ *In some cases a buyer is not given any service until he or she is able to prove the ability to make the purchase. That can include a letter from the buyer's banker, acknowledging how much money the buyer has to work with. It also can include a resume that outlines the buyer's background and experience. This information is required by some business sales professionals.*

❖ *Patience for a buyer can mean refusing to remove contingencies in an agreement until all questions have been answered; every bit of confusion has been cleared. An impatient buyer, eager to get through due diligence before completing the process runs the risk of being committed to a deal for a business that is not as it was represented to be.*

❖ *It's not uncommon for a business owner to have the business on the market six months before getting an acceptable offer.*

❖ *For many buyers, it may take a year or more to find and purchase the "right" business*

CHAPTER TWO

PREPARATION FOR SELLERS

So, you've decided to sell your small business. You plan to announce that it is available for purchase – discreetly of course – and then you'll prepare yourself for the onslaught of questions and offers.

One fact you should know at the outset is that the initial appearance of your small business when it's presented for sale can determine whether or not things will go well as it is reviewed and considered by potential buyers. Making a good first impression is vital. Just as important is that it can stand up under scrutiny.

Prospective purchasers are quick to dismiss any offering that doesn't seem quite ready for presentation. If the information is not complete or if some of the facts don't make sense, an offering will probably be rejected without further analysis. Buyers, at least most of them, are cautious and a bit cynical. After all, the purchase of a business can be among the most important decisions in a person's life. At risk may be their life savings, along with the years of work and sacrifice devoted to succeeding in the business and securing their financial well being. A mistake can be disastrous.

Is it any wonder then, that a typical buyer does not readily accept all of a seller's claims? Most buyers also are cautious about any business not presented in its entirety. If the seller can't answer all questions, or provide complete accounting information for the past three or five years, the buyer assumes there is information purposely being held back.

In addition to exercising some healthy cynicism, buyers usually apply logic, working out the arguments for and against their acquisition of what you offer. They even use a bit of intuition as they examine various small business opportunities and consider what might be a good fit.

"Could I really do this?" "How does this feel?" "Are these people being honest with me?" These are some of the questions that pop into the buyer's mind, demanding answers, before he or she wants to go forward in the investigation of a possible acquisition.

You may notice that a prospective buyer is listening and asking questions, but also looking intensely around your office, and the facility, eager to observe any clues and collect any information that can be gleaned about the business. And as the buyer's questions come out, it may feel to you more like an interrogation than a question and answer session, with the prospect prepared to catch you in a misstatement.

So if you make a claim that you can't support, even if the failure results from an honest error; or if you subject someone to a process of due diligence that goes on too long and is too complicated, even if the facts are all there, you may wind up scaring away a good buyer. Forever.

And for no reason other than the fact that you weren't prepared.

That means the time to resolve problems and answer questions that might surface – to iron out any kinks in the offering – is before the first buyer has a chance to review it. Don't wait till you're well into the process.

As one business broker puts it: "Once you start back pedaling, you're in trouble."

Even though we're not yet talking in detail about the stage where you're meeting with buyers – that part comes later in the book – it's important that sellers understand from the beginning, how critical it is that you are fully prepared when your enterprise goes on the block.

Rather than drag out your offering over a period of several months, changing the price every so often, and waiting for buyer comments and questions before deciding what information to collect and present, it's best to consider that you have a brief window to strut your business stuff. In my experience, the first 30 to 60 days after a small business goes on the market may be the most critical time.

Here's a review of some of ways you can be prepared when your business is introduced for sale.

What You Probably Thought of Already: Books/Records, Equipment List, Profile

Books/records

Most buyers of small businesses feel that a three year financial history is sufficient to gain a solid understanding about the company's recent performance. I feel that providing a five-year history is even better. Along with a P&L and balance sheet covering the prior calendar or fiscal years, it's advisable to provide this information for the current year, as up to date as possible.

Depending on the size of the business and sophistication of the market in which it functions, you may be wise to provide financials information subjected to a full review. The cost ($5,000 or more) is an unneeded expense if you are selling a business at a price under about $500,000. And it helps if your enterprise is in an industry about which there is a great deal of standard information available, so a buyer can readily determine if the performance of your business is typical. You also are at an advantage, in terms of the financial detail required by a buyer, if you are selling a franchised business. The operating figures you provide to the franchisor are generally considered reliable reports, particularly if the buyer has the opportunity to talk with the franchisor, and verify numbers from your operation.

As the asking price goes beyond $1,000,000, it's more likely that your buyers will want to know that your operating statements have been subjected to a formal financial review. That's because of the larger sums at stake, and because the buyer for a business that size is likely to be more sophisticated and accustomed to working with carefully scrutinized information.

Simpler and less costly businesses usually can be properly represented, to the satisfaction of most buyers, with figures compiled as a result of less thorough and extensive procedures.

While buyers initially are provided with P&Ls and balance sheets covering three or five years, you may be asked, as you get into a sales agreement, to furnish the level of detail that allows buyers to verify the accuracy of your numbers. That means a seller is well advised to be ready to produce invoices, sales reports, accounts receivables aging schedules and other documentation that goes into the entries contained in your month-end reports.

Other supporting documents, such as depreciation schedules, payroll records and bank registers might also be requested and should be made available. But all of this detail is too much for an initial introduction of your business and we'll get to the way to "stage" the information later in this chapter.

Assets list

The depreciation schedule is a great place to start if you're assembling a list of equipment. You want to include all of your capital equipment, as well as office furniture, fixtures, and even leasehold improvements. Pull as much information together as possible, including acquisition cost and date, service contracts and records, and even appraisals. A used equipment dealer involved in your industry may be willing to give you some idea of valuation at a nominal cost.

Any vehicles to be included in the sale can be listed separately, showing their Blue Book value, mileage, accessories and so forth.

While it's a good idea to conduct an inventory of parts, supplies and finished goods at the outset, you can do it quickly to get an approximate value. A more detailed inventory will probably be conducted when you close a sale and require an exact dollar figure.

Copies of your lease – or leases if there are multiple locations, customer contracts, franchise agreements, deals established with employees and similar documentation can be considered assets of the business as well. These should be assembled and photocopied for presentation to a prospective buyer at the appropriate time.

Business Profile

How long has your enterprise been in business? How long have you owned it? How many employees? How many years remaining on the lease, and at what rental? These and other basic facts about the business should be presented in a one or two-page profile that can be shown to interested buyers as a first step in the introduction of your business.

Some business owners feel competent to prepare this document themselves while others feel it's worth a few hundred dollars to have this material prepared by a professional copy writer. And many business sellers, brokers and agents believe it's useful to add a page that describes the market in which your business functions, with an emphasis on the growth prospects. Back this up with any recent newspaper or trade magazine articles that talk about the glowing future of your industry and the growth anticipated in the market for your products and services. Such outside materials add credibility to your positive projections.

A one-page summary of your company's financial performance belongs with this package. It needn't go into the details of operations, just review the income, as up to date as possible for the current year, as well as for prior years, and a recount of the totals in the main categories of expenses. Balance sheet summaries also can be included.

Many business brokers encourage their clients, or even help them, to prepare a page of "recast" financials. If you notice expense items that would not be incurred by a new owner (such as your car lease and country club membership), and if you feel that your successor – more active in the business than you are – could operate with lower labor costs, this is the place to document the dollar value of these differences. Show how the bottom line will be increased by adding back your personal expenses and deducting those costs that you have, but won't necessarily be incurred by the buyer.

Incidentally, while I think that recasting financials is a powerful tool in presenting a business to a prospective buyer, I fear its misuse in the way it is conveyed to the buyer. Be sure to include a disclaimer on the same page that describes the recast financial information. Note that the recast is your opinion not a representation or promise that the buyer will enjoy exactly the financial results depicted.

Another section of this profile might be a description of the ideal buyer. Suppose you use your electrical engineering experience in your business, and you recommend that the new owner have much the same background. A prospect who is similarly qualified may be more intrigued upon learning about this. And a prospect who lacks the capability will decline to pursue your offering, saving you time in the process.

And if you're aware of negative factors that might affect the future of your enterprise it's advisable to state them in writing on a page called "disclosure notice." This page needn't be generally circulated, but should be available for judicious use.

For a useful tool that can help you put together an effective business profile, go to this Internet address: *www.USABizMart.com* and download the Business Profile form. The site also is a resource for services that can help you prepare the business profile. (Please see the business profile sample at the end of Chapter 8).

Staging

Of course, just because you've assembled all of this material and information does not mean you're required to hand it to everyone who thinks they may have an interest in your business. Rather, the common procedure is to distribute this data in "stages," matching the interest level of a prospective buyer with a suitable amount of information.

In Stage One, a buyer learns about the availability of your business and can have preliminary questions addressed with a single page "blind" profile, a form that reviews some of the particulars but does not include the name of your company or any identifying details. (Please see the "blind" profile sample at the end of chapter 8).

If this sparks an interest on the part of the buyer, who now wants additional information, the next step is usually to obtain a signature on a non-disclosure agreement, whereby the buyer pledges to respect and observe the confidentiality of any information about your offering that is provided.

The Stage Two materials, for those who've signed non-disclosure agreements, can include the profile on the business along with the summary of your company's financial information for the past three or five years. This might also be a good time to release the "disclosure notice" mentioned above, so the buyer is formally informed about any possible problems you anticipate in the future operation of the business.

Stage Three information is typically everything else that a buyer may want to see, but is predicated on an accepted offer, or at least an acceptable letter of intent for the buyer to purchase your business.

At this stage – the time for what is called "due diligence" – the buyer will have gained a fairly thorough overview about your business and will want to look into the specifics to deepen his or her understanding. The due diligence analysis is also the buyer's opportunity to verify the accuracy of the information provided in the earlier stages.

The buyer may engage the services of an accountant to go over the financials in more detail and compare your daily records with the summary contained in the balance sheets and profit and loss reports. Also, an attorney may be asked to review your property lease and other contracts and agreements. The purpose of this investigation is to make certain there are no undisclosed problems which the buyer feels will negatively impact the business in the future. The buyer's examination of these documents is also intended to verify that the information provided in earlier stages is supported by the detailed records.

Trial Run

In the process of preparing your business profile and organizing your financial information and other documents, you might want to pretend that you are a prospective buyer and actually go through a session of your own due diligence. Is every statement made in the business profile supported by the documentation? When the buyer reviews the financials, will materials such as the receivables aging reports, the payroll ledgers and the check register yield the exact same information as reported on the summaries?

If there are discrepancies, this is the time to become aware of them and make sure you have a correct explanation, or make changes to the profile so it corresponds to the facts. And double check everything, including the simple math that was used in the summary sheets. If there is a math error, you may know it is a simple mistake and nothing more. But the buyer is likely to suspect that the mistake in addition, or in subtraction, is proof you've been tinkering with the numbers to produce a better outcome than the reality, and failed to cover your tracks sufficiently.

If all the information is true and accurate, the computations should be perfect. That's the reasoning of most buyers. So, if there is a problem with the math – the thinking goes – it's indicative of some plot to misrepresent the business and to confuse, or lie to the buyer.

Without the preparatory step of a trial run, you may be surprised to learn that inconsistencies exist in your reporting – inconsistencies which will be uncovered by the buyer. And while you're scratching your head and saying: "Gee, I didn't know about that," the buyer is likely to begin wondering if there are other "surprises," perhaps better hidden than what was uncovered. That's usually the moment when the buyer experiences a sense of distrust that can easily culminate in a "no sale."

Assemble Your Team

The final step in the category of obvious preparations is to make sure you have your experts in place, ready to help you when needed. As noted above, you might call on your attorney to review and to go over with you the basics of your lease or other agreements. And your accounting professional will be helpful in preparing a presentation of recast financial information. It may also be useful to obtain a business valuation from a qualified business broker or appraiser. And perhaps you'll engage an advertising expert to help plan your marketing campaign and to prepare the business profile that goes into the selling package (the collection of materials presented to interested and qualified buyers.)

Why So Many Deals Fail

Poor preparation is a key factor in the failures that occur to more than half of the deals that begin with an accepted offer.

Following the advice offered earlier in this chapter will help you prevent a number of these problems, by eliminating any surprises the buyer might encounter when moving into the due diligence phase of a transaction. Though initially skeptical, most buyers become more trusting if they discover consistency in the information as their examination of business records proceeds. And that's a healthy sign that your deal is going to hold together through completion.

But the preparation and assembly of written material and documentation is only half your job as you get your business ready for sale.

What You May Not Have Anticipated:
Meeting with Landlord, Approvals, Transfer of Licenses

Even a profitable, well run business with impeccable records can be rejected by buyers and ignored by business brokers if all of the components needed to operate cannot be included in the sale. Sometimes it is just simple things – not handled on a timely basis – that ruin the chances for a healthy small business to get matched up with a qualified and willing buyer.

Lease

An estimated twenty five percent of would-be business sales agreements have smashed up on the rocks over the past few years at the very point that a seller took a buyer to meet the land owner. And that doesn't factor in the cases in which the problems at that juncture were actually resolved, and the deal saved by a renegotiated lease or restructured deal – usually costly to the seller.

For retail businesses, including restaurants and many personal service enterprises, location is a key component of success. If there is a short time remaining on the lease and little likelihood of getting a new rental agreement or extension of the current one, the business will have little market value. Certainly the enterprise is worth much more with a long-term lease in place than a short one. The saleability of a location-dependent operation is also impacted if the landlord chooses – and has legal standing – to withhold consent to assignment of the leasehold interest from seller to buyer.

Sellers of location-sensitive businesses certainly understand the importance of a good lease. Yet often they're reluctant to work to insure that they'll be able to satisfy this requirement in their offering.

"It's too early to talk to the landlady," is a typical comment. "Let's see if we get a good buyer, then we'll deal with the lease," is another.

And it's somewhat understandable that a business owner is reluctant to open the issue. There's the concern that talking to the landlord will force the cat out of the bag, causing the rumor mill to work overtime with discussions about exactly the topic which the seller would like to keep confidential – that is, the fact that the business is up for sale.

Then there's the worry that once your landlord knows you're planning to leave, he'll somehow feel betrayed, with the result of worsened relations between business owner and landlord. As any business operator knows, you've got enough troubles running a successful company without adding the problem of bad relations with the person to whom you send the monthly rent checks.

Despite these and related concerns, however, the best strategy invariably is to discuss your plans with the landlord before the business is officially on the market. Even if there's a major portion of eternity remaining on the lease, and a clear formula setting the rent well into the future, you should contact the person who owns the property where you conduct your business. Let him know there may be a new tenant in his future. Get his reaction. If he's got problems with that idea, work with your landlord to get the issues resolved.

Will the new business owner need to meet a minimum standard of experience and financial solvency to satisfy the landlord? What is that standard? Are you going to have to remain on the lease and pay the rent if the buyer falls behind? Are you willing to do that? Do you need to get your lawyer involved to make sure you have solid rights of assignability under the lease? Will it take legal action to enforce those rights? Is that a cause you are willing to pursue?

It is these and similar questions that need to be posed so the solutions are incorporated into the business offering when it goes on the market. For example, a poor lease may mean the business is offered with a low down payment so the buyer can retain some of the capital needed to finance a move.

Though it's tempting and it seems reasonable to put off the frustrating exercise of lease negotiations until it's an absolute must – when a specific buyer is waiting for the outcome, that's actually the worst time. While the buyer is wondering when there might be some resolution, he or she is likely to have second thoughts. That's when buyers typically find another business that is all ready to be taken over. You can eliminate those risks by working out the lease details before hand.

Having lease terms spelled out applies even if you own the property and plan to keep it, leasing some or all to the new business owner. Establish the terms of the lease you want to provide. Then make them part of the package.

And if you own your business as a franchisee, with the lease belonging to the franchisor, your job is somewhat simplified. In most cases the approval from franchise head-quarters for you to proceed with your sale will include an okay for the lease transfer to an acceptable buyer.

Other agreements

The idea of having things worked out from the time the business goes on the market should be applied also to equipment leases, employment contracts, franchise obligations, purchase agreements covering your equipment, deals with customers, advertising orders and any other written – sometimes even verbal – contracts that you rely on to conduct business.

If you have entered into any agreement that provides service for your business, or ties you to a customer, you need to make sure that whoever wants to buy and to operate your business will be able to count on those same agreements. That may mean talking to your lawyer to determine the transferability of these understandings. And it may mean going to vendors or customers to make sure they'll accept the new owner of the business on the same terms they took you.

Agreements you've made with any of your employees should be handled the same way. Dealing with this issue can require the finesse of a career diplomat, but there are strategies for approaching the problem and you can ask your advisors – business broker or attorney – for advice. One solution, for example, is to take key employees into your confidence, let them known what is planned, and promise that once a successful sale is completed, they will be rewarded for keeping your secret and for their willingness to cooperate with a new owner.

I can't stress enough the importance of caution in the way this is handled, as this strategy backfired when I offered a business I was selling to a key employee. He immediately alerted the other employees about the impending sale, and this knowledge impacted operations – and not to the benefit of my business.

Licenses and permits

And don't forget the importance to the buyer of those clearances you've obtained from local, county and state governing bodies, over the years, to conduct your business and operate your equipment.

If you're the owner of any food business offering alcoholic beverages, you know your buyer may be required to apply for your alcoholic beverage license from an agency of the state. This is mandated in most states, and ordinarily in the sale of such a business, the seller's license is transferred to the new owner after payment of a fee and submission of an application by the buyer, along with an investigation by the state.

Want to make sure the license transfer doesn't become a problem in your deal? Inform prospective buyers about what is required by the state at the earliest part of the introduction to the business. Provide the forms and let them know there'll be an investigation to learn where the purchase money came from, and to determine if any buyers have a business or personal connection with persons the state considers "undesirable."

If an eager buyer suddenly gets second thoughts when learning about this procedure, you'll be glad you were in a position to find that out. Now you can send the person on their way and spend your time with those buyers who are willing and able to make a deal.

And just because the business you want to sell is not regulated in this manner, doesn't mean you escape the concern about government approval. If, for example, you use an air compressor, such as in an auto repair garage, or welding equipment of the type employed in say, a machine shop, you'd better learn what local regulators require for your buyer to do, in order to operate the business with the same equipment. You may learn that no permits or clearances are needed. But in many communities in the United States there are regulations covering these matters. And what if the rules are much more stringent than they were when you received the needed approvals?

There are a number of strategies that you and your buyer can employ to smooth the transition in cases where there are special and difficult approvals required. Whether it's the simple precaution of talking to the landlord beforehand, or a complicated tactic, such as using a corporate entity to work around a license transfer issue, the time to anticipate potential problems and deal killers and then work out solutions, is before, not after you've obtained a buyer.

It also is a solid idea for you to be prepared, at this point, with the parts of the deal that you're to perform. Are you willing to train? For how long? During what hours? Does the buyer get your covenant not to compete? What are the terms, and how much of the value of the business do you place on the covenant?

Also, how is the purchase price to be allocated? How much for goodwill? How will the tangible assets be valued?

Spring cleaning

This also is the best time – before offering your business for sale – to handle the unfinished business. Collect or write off your old receivables. If you're in the middle of a stalled legal dispute, try to get it resolved one way or another. If you're on notice to clean up a hazardous deposit or remove a public nuisance, there's no time like the present to make sure that matter is taken care of, once and for all. Even if you're not thrilled with what has to be done, it's worth doing now, rather than later. It'll free you up to deal with the next stage of your business life. And it will allow you to present your business free of difficulties and entanglements.

Financing Preparation

Another bit of spade work you can do at this point has to do with lining up sources of cash the buyer can use to help with purchase price and working capital. You may want to talk to your bank, to find out if it can provide a purchase loan, how much can be lent, what security will be required (business assets or personal property, or both), and what qualifications will be required of the buyer.

One financing resource that definitely is worth investigating can be accessed at *www.bizbuyfinancing.com*. Find out if yours is one of the many businesses that can be financed at competitive rates and with quick service designed particularly for needs of owners of small businesses. If so, you can begin the prequalification process for your business so that a loan to help with its purchase can more readily be applied for and more quickly obtained.

The topic of financing a purchase will get more attention in a subsequent chapter, and is noted here to be added to your planning checklist.

Delays Kill Deals

If this seems like a lot of preparatory work, before you even have a real, breathing buyer lined up, you should know that once you find that buyer you will run the risk of losing him or her if your agreement runs into snags, delays and problems. Your best strategy is to handle, beforehand, all of the tasks and responsibilities you'll have to do anyway. Get as much completed as possible before the business is even offered and you can reduce the danger that occurs during the due diligence period – after there's an accepted offer – if there are unanticipated troubles and unresolved matters that cause deal killing delays.

Conclusion

The smart seller knows that the best way to complete a deal, once an interested buyer is engaged, is to plan ahead to eliminate those nasty, deal killing surprises. Some business brokers estimate that surprises account for nearly all of the 50% of agreements on small business sales that ultimately fall apart.

Yes, it's more work for you, but it's definitely in your best interests as a seller to find out what will be required for ownership transfer, and then do as much as possible to pave the way for the person who's interested in taking over the company – even before that person surfaces.

Sometimes the preparatory work reviewed in this chapter is the hardest part of selling. It may also be the difference between achieving, and failing to achieve, a satisfactory transaction to sell your small business.

KEY POINTS FROM THIS CHAPTER

❖ *Considering that purchase of a business is a critical, life-changing move for most buyers, and that their future financial well-being is in the balance, it isn't surprising that they are cautious and skeptical about the business opportunities they view.*

❖ *Your careful preparation when your business is offered for sale will substantially improve your chances of a deal at a fair and realistic price and terms. By contrast, lack of preparation is a major reason that 50% of accepted offers never make it through the due diligence examination to a successful close.*

❖ *"Once you start backpedaling, you're in trouble." This good advice is a reminder to make sure you have solid facts to support the statements about your business.*

❖ *Preparation of a business prospectus (also known as the offering package) with financials and assets lists, before the marketing effort begins, will allow you to respond promptly to interested buyers who need more information.*

❖ *Don't spend the first 30 to 60 days of your marketing campaign – the most critical time – trying to "get your act together." With all needed materials already assembled and in a package for qualified buyer prospects, you can turn your attention to the important responsibilities of interacting with buyers, responding to questions that are raised during the marketing, refining strategy and shaping your offering in response to market feedback, staying fully involved in the company to make sure its performance doesn't lag, and handling other tasks needed to sell your business.*

❖ *Can you get an appraisal or "statement of value" performed on your equipment? It helps to educate prospective buyers about what is being offered.*

❖ *Having your financial information analyzed in an accounting review is advisable for larger businesses (with selling prices above $500,000) and those with more complicated financial structures.*

❖ *The inclusion of "recast" financials with your P&L, helps the buyer understand how earnings might add up under his or her ownership.*

❖ *Assemble and photocopy all written agreements important to the business, such as premises lease, advertising contracts and any customer, vendor or employee contracts so they can be provided to qualified buyer prospects.*

❖ A two-page business profile giving a bit of the history and details of your operation is a useful addition to the business prospectus.

❖ A useful tool for putting together a business profile is a Business Profile form available on the internet at www.USABizMart.com

❖ Look for resources at www.USA.BizMart.com to help you with your business profile if you don't feel you have the time or background to produce it yourself.

❖ Including a description of the ideal buyer in the business prospectus helps to rule out unqualified buyers and save your time. It also might encourage those who qualify to further investigate your offering.

❖ Also include in the business prospectus an explanation of opportunities for growth and added profits that might await the new owner. Are there any newspaper or magazine articles that confirm your positive predictions by referring to the expansion in your industry or geographic area? If so, attach copies of these to your statement.

❖ Don't forget to include copies of marketing materials, ads, flyers, brochures and coupons in your business prospectus.

❖ Providing a serious buyer with a notice about problems you anticipate for the business, if any, helps to weed out those prospects for whom the problem is a deal killer. As the person would have discovered the negative information in due diligence, and then might have backed out of the deal, early disclosure of possible problems helps to prevent wasting time with the wrong buyers.

❖ Staging is the process of providing a level of information about the business that corresponds to a buyer's degree of interest. The first stage is a basic overview without identifying the company. Interim stages involve the disclosure of additional financial and other details to a buyer who is qualified and wants to further investigate the business. The final stage occurs after an agreement between buyer and seller for a transaction, subject to the buyer being satisfied with examination of all additional information. During this due diligence stage, the smart seller complies with most every reasonable request from the buyer for added details about the business.

❖ *A trial run is conducted by a seller who rehearses the review of information that will be conducted by a buyer. The purpose is to make sure that all the material is clear, accurate and consistent, so there are no surprises when the buyer is engaged in the due diligence process.*

❖ *Assembling your professional team, including broker, attorney and accountant, is best done before the business is marketed. These professionals should understand their role, be familiar with what you are trying to accomplish and be prepared to assist. You might want to add to this group, an advertising specialist to help with parts of your business prospectus, such as the business profile.*

❖ *Details about terms of sale offered, including the allocation of purchase price, training agreement and seller's covenant not to compete, should be worked out before the offering hits the market. In this way, the seller guards against the possibility that uncertainty about these matters will slow the progress of the transaction.*

❖ *Dealing with the landlord, franchisor, equipment leasing companies and others whose approval is needed to transfer assets of the business, should be done prior to offering the business for sale. Any problems should be resolved beforehand so that disruptions or surprises are eliminated or minimized.*

❖ *While it also might be a good idea to talk to key employees about the impending sale – in order to get their assistance, perhaps with an incentive for their discretion and cooperation – this plan should only be implemented if you're fairly certain the employee(s) can be trusted with the information.*

❖ *Preventing surprises and delays also means determining what licenses and permits need to be transferred and then, when possible, getting started on those processes.*

❖ *Preparation must include doing what's necessary to resolve legal disputes and to comply with orders from governmental agencies. In other words, any unfinished business that hangs over your company will cause buyer questions and jeopardize your deal. It should be dispatched, as much as possible, before your business is offered for sale.*

❖ *An important job in the process of preparation is to arrange for financing, so the buyer will have assistance raising the money to complete the deal. This includes finding out what qualifications the buyer will need to get the loan. Such "pre-approval" helps a deal move forward by supplying needed cash and reflects well on the business when it's first presented. The business's image is enhanced by willingness of a financial institution to lend on it.*

❖ *Check out www.bizbuyfinancing.com for information about a financing resource that is designed specifically for small businesses in the U.S. Here you can pre-qualify your business for a loan to help with the purchase when you find a qualified buyer.*

❖ *And remember that an important reason for your preparation is so that you can return your focus to operations of your business – on making sure it continues to run smoothly and efficiently – once it goes on the market.*

❖ *Another important reason for your preparation is that delays kill deals. The fewer opportunities there are for your agreement to start stuttering over issues, questions and problems that could have been taken care of beforehand, the more likely you'll see your accepted offer result in a completed transaction.*

CHAPTER THREE

BUYER PREPARATION IS VITAL TO SUCCESS

"I'm sure there are more difficult things in life than trying to buy a business I just don't know what they might be."

That's the way one buyer explained his year-and-a-half campaign – he called it a "crusade" – to purchase a small business. The crusade ended successfully when he took over a custom cabinet shop from the founder who was ready to retire after over 40 years in business. And the buyer was right, it wasn't easy.

Still, his assessment may not be accurate; buying a business is not among the most difficult challenges in life. But it is a demanding task filled with frustrations and disappointments, and no guarantee of success. Buyers who've finally discovered a suitable company they were able to purchase, have reported conducting their searches for periods that often exceed a year, and sometimes require more than two years.

Among the factors making this such a challenging project is the simple reality of demand and supply. More people want to purchase a business with a history of earnings and a positive future than there are available companies fitting that description. Also making this a hard endeavor are the offerings of businesses that seem appealing at first glance but don't maintain that appeal once they are looked at carefully.

And the buyer's search is further complicated by the discovery of unreasonable sellers offering good businesses. Sellers who have an inflated idea about the value of their companies are the other side of the "unrealistic buyers" coin. Some sellers think they'll get more than their business' value from a buyer who has more cash than common sense. The way this plays out is that you'll have your time wasted with business offerings that just don't compute when you examine the numbers. At the right price the math would work out fine; you'd get a reasonable return so you can take a salary and pay off any debt incurred to make the purchase. And sometimes you can wait until a seller comes back "down to Earth." I've seen that strategy employed. But you may not want to have anything to do now, or later, with someone who has insulted you by expecting you to be a sucker.

Buyers who become discouraged after they discover – yet again – that a business which looked so promising is, in fact, a losing proposition, would do well to adjust their disappointment threshold, perhaps become a little more cynical, if they're going to continue the search.

You, the buyer, need to learn – if you haven't already – that the cycle of high hopes followed by sad reality is really just part of the buying process. And you need to continue, undaunted, with your search.

As was suggested in the first chapter, the business buyer most likely to enjoy a successful conclusion for the search campaign is someone focused on finding a healthy business with a good future and a reasonable seller. Your expectations, if they are based on realities of the market and the willingness to pay a fair price and terms, will lead you to a business to buy which meets your criteria – that is if you invest enough time and effort.

If, however, you conceive of your search as a contest to see who's smarter, quicker and more deceptive – you or the seller – you'll be likely to engage in lots of negotiations, tinged with anger and bad feelings, but without a suitable business to show for your efforts.

Can you regard the search as a collaborative effort? You'll be working with your team – lawyer, accountant and broker(s) or agent(s) – and with a seller to reach a mutually desirable goal. Put the idea of cooperation and communication at the foundation of your strategy, and you're most likely to be successful.

Communications

Well prepared buyers, in addition to working with realistic expectations, are ready to communicate about what they are looking for – their search criteria – as well as about what they are ready to bring to the right deal. Having been involved in hundreds of transactions – as a buyer, a seller or a broker – I can speak from substantial experience about the frustrations that come up when trying to do business with someone who won't reveal any information about what he or she wants, or has to offer.

As one seller said about an uncooperative buyer: "That guy thinks he's so clever because he's playing his cards close to his chest. He wants me to talk but he's not willing to let me know where he's coming from. I don't know if he's interested or qualified. I don't know if he's even someone I want to do business with."

And he added this point: "There are plenty of good buyers for my business – buyers who are up front about where they stand. I don't have time to play cat-and-mouse games with someone who may not even be serious."

Preparing to be a good communicator also involves setting up the mechanics you'll need to receive information and to respond quickly. A dedicated phone line – preferably a mobile phone that will reach you anywhere – along with a fax and a dedicated email address are recommended. This way you and your team members are in a position to exchange information quickly and securely. And make sure an answering machine or voice mail is connected to your phone lines so you don't miss any important messages. By being prepared to communicate effectively you send a message to those with whom you are working. They'll know that you're serious and ready to do business.

Don't be one of those buyers whose 4-year-old answers the phone when a broker is calling to tell you about a situation, new on the market, that might be just what you want. Being prepared so you can exchange information efficiently with team members and with a seller, once you're negotiating, makes it easy for them to conduct business with you. And maintaining good communications increases the chances of your success as a buyer.

Assemble Team

I know of cases where circumstances such as the one described above – a child picks up the phone and sings nursery rhymes to the person calling to tell a buyer about a hot tip on a business – have seriously hampered a buyer's efforts. A similar kind of breakdown occurs when you are one of several prospective buyers for a terrific business, but not in a position to have the financials reviewed or to have a letter of intent drawn up, because you haven't yet established your relationship with the professionals you need to help with the effort.

An important part of your preparation is to interview attorneys – to find one who has experience in business purchases, and to meet with the various accountants you've heard about so you can determine who is best able to quickly examine the books of a small business and report to you on its condition. You're looking for professionals who are competent at their work, will charge you reasonable rates and – equally important – are people with whom you can work productively. This will, again, require good communication on your end so the working relationship with your advisors gets the desired results with quick turnaround.

Also part of your team should be a few brokers and agents who are in touch with the market of business offerings and can let you know what is available. There's somewhat of an art in dealing with the professionals in business brokerage and we'll get into that subject in more detail in a subsequent chapter. The key point for this discussion is that you want to meet with these people as one of the early steps in your preparation, so they are working on your behalf, trying to find the right business for you to buy. And your good communication with them will enable them to understand what you want and don't want.

Many buyers contact brokers and agents only in response to business-for-sale ads these professionals have listed. If that's your only mode of reaching business sales people, and then you simply ask a few questions and respond to their queries with the predictable comments: "Not interested" or "I'll think about it and let you know if I'm interested," you're not likely to establish a working rapport with any of those brokers and agents. That means your phone number will not be entered on their lists of people to contact about interesting new business offerings.

My recommendation is that you interview brokers and agents as you would attorneys and accountants. The difference is that you will work with a single attorney and one accountant, but may find yourself dealing with a few brokers and agents to help you find a business to buy.

Your Acquisition Resume

And what's one of the first things on the agenda when you meet with a broker or agent? It should be to let them know, with as many specifics as possible, exactly what you are seeking. The best way to do that is with the acquisition resume. It provides a business sales professional with both your criteria and your capabilities in writing, within a single, well organized document.

Does that seem like a lot of trouble? It really is not. You need to collect all your thoughts on this subject anyway. There's probably no better means of communicating what you want and can offer than your acquisition resume.

And I can tell you from the standpoint of the business broker that a document like this will help you immeasurably in gaining the attention and the allegiance of the people with whom you are working. All they have to do is refer to your document to know exactly what will work for you and also to be reminded that you are a favored buyer. That's because you are organized, communicative and clear about objectives.

Similar to the resume used in looking for a job, your acquisition resume will start with the objective and explain the general type and size of business that you seek. Then it can cover, in more detail, some of the businesses you might like. You can make a list of suitable kinds of companies, and note the industries that will work, as well as your preference for retail, manufacturing, wholesale distribution, food service or some types of personal or business service firms. How many employees do you want to manage? Are you interested in a business that is open on the weekends? These are topics you should be thinking about and be prepared to note on your document. And be sure to include a list or an explanation of what you don't want. This will make your search criteria even more useful and will help avoid time-wasting introductions to businesses that don't meet your interests or needs.

Make sure your acquisition resume provides details about your financial requirements and what size company you are capable of purchasing.

Also in this document you can review your work history and experience, so that anyone reading it would know what you are capable of managing.

The acquisition resume isn't the only part of your campaign that will have similarities to a job search. Many of the things you would do if hunting for a position with a company, governmental agency or other organization, you will do when looking for the right business. It's important, for example, that you make it a habit to network with people who might be able to help, that you pursue all interesting – even just moderately interesting – opportunities, and that you work consistently at your objective until it is realized.

Remember that there are more buyers for good business opportunities than there are good businesses. The market dynamics are similar to that of pursuing a job along with other candidates. As in a job search, the hunt for your business entails a great deal of preparation and forethought.

Financial Preparation

Among the important items on the acquisition resume is a declaration of the amount of money you are prepared to put into a deal. Let your business sales professionals and any prospective sellers know what you have for a down payment and working capital. And this is the time to decide, and then declare, what personal assets you will use, if any, to secure an obligation incurred as a result of the seller financing part of a deal. If you're adamantly set against anything other than assets of the business being used as collateral for the seller's loan, you should be aware that this will reduce your desirability as a buyer, and limit the number of offerings to which you'll be introduced. You may be thinking that "it depends on the deal." And maybe this indecision helps keep you in your comfort zone. But it doesn't let those with whom you are working know what you are willing to do to get a business. And it makes their job harder.

Incidentally, you don't always have to cover the full amount of the obligation to the seller with collateral. Sometimes he or she will be satisfied with a second trust deed on your home for an amount of say, half the note, with the other half collateralized with assets of the company you are purchasing. Maybe you are willing to do more. Or less. You determine the limits of what you're willing and able to do, and that should be revealed as part of your acquisition resume. And regardless of your limits it is important that those invited to do business with you – as your representatives or as the other party in your transaction – are informed of exactly your capabilities and what you are willing to do.

A lender letter is a useful addition to your acquisition resume. Speak to your business bank to determine how much money it might be willing to lend, based on your assets, credit history and the type of business you are intending to purchase. You may learn that the bank is not prepared to make a commitment, and certainly without information about the business.

For a pre-approval, a good choice is to go to the *www.bizbuyfinancing.com* site. This lending source is specifically designed to aid in the purchase of small businesses and, as such, is prepared to help buyers navigate the rapidly changing requirements and financing availability that potential buyers experience in the marketplace for business acquisition funding.

Time is of the Essence

And while a buyer is getting prepared it never hurts to remind himself or herself of the adage that says time is of the essence. Acting quickly and responding decisively can mean the difference between getting the business you want and just missing out on what would have been a great opportunity. So make sure you are prepared to move on any possibility that comes up when you get that phone call in the canned goods aisle of your grocery store, or on the way to your kids' soccer practice or, at the place where you're working until you can find your business and quit the job.

I'm familiar with several situations involving a lost opportunity due to lack of preparation on the part of a buyer – both mental and in terms of the technology needed to communicate promptly and effectively. That's why I advocate the dedicated phone line, the use of message management tools (voice mail or a phone answering system), and even a fax that you can use to send and receive documents in a hurry. Most of the time, a fax machine in your study is simply a dust catching eyesore, incongruent with the rest of the decor in the room. But when you're in the middle of competitive negotiations, the machine's ability to get the seller's information to you and to transmit your letter of intent to her in a few minutes, makes it a most blessed instrument of your victory.

Conclusion

Due to a number of factors: The supply and demand imbalance in favor of the seller, the sense of frustration that can set in after a string of disappointments, the number of unsuitable or improperly priced businesses offered, and the unrealistic expectations of many buyers, the discovery and purchase of a desirable small business is a difficult project to complete successfully. Buyers are advised to be prepared so the quest can be managed effectively. Included in the preparatory steps are assembling a team of support professionals (including attorney, accountant and business sales professionals), putting together an acquisition resume, getting organized with respect to the cash that will be available and might be raised, and being ready and equipped to move quickly if necessary.

KEY POINTS FROM THIS CHAPTER

❖ *The purchase of a profitable small business with a promising future at a fair price can be a difficult task to complete, due in part to the fact there are more buyers than there are satisfactory businesses on the market.*

❖ *The other side of the "unreasonable buyers" coin are sellers who hope to catch someone willing to meet an excessive asking price. This factor, and the presence of totally unsuitable businesses that should not be offered because they don't make economic sense, can cause a great deal of frustration on the part of buyers who aren't ready for the disappointments that come with this process.*

❖ *Buyers who wish to be successful at finding and purchasing a suitable business are urged to communicate effectively with advisors, business sales professionals and sellers. Those who don't explain precisely what they want and what they can do, will be unable to build the alliances and trust needed to reach their objective.*

❖ *Part of communicating well is having the mechanics in place, including a mobile phone, a way to receive and to easily access phone messages, and a fax machine readily available.*

❖ *The time to build your team of professionals – attorney, accountant and business sales professionals – is at the beginning of your search. That way you won't be caught un-prepared if you need to move quickly on an interesting deal.*

❖ *The acquisition resume, which details a buyer's search criteria as well as his or her capabilities – financial and otherwise – is a very effective way to communicate with brokers, agents and sellers. It should include what the buyer is not interested in so as to be as explicit as possible.*

❖ *Buyers are well advised to provide some detail of their financial strength, including how much cash is available for down payment and working capital, how much in the way of assets will be used as collateral for seller financing (assuming the buyer is willing to pledge, for example, some real estate equity), and how much might be obtained in a loan if the deal is acceptable to the lender.*

❖ For pre-approval in the rapidly changing world of lending sources for small business purchases, perhaps the best resource is found at www.bizbuyfinancing.com The lenders working through this site are specialists with innovative programs to help small business buyers complete their purchases.

❖ The search for a good business to buy can be compared to a job search. There are more good candidates to buy a business than there are suitable businesses, just as there may be several applicants for a position with a company, government agency or other organization.

❖ Time is of the essence in many cases when buyers are competing for a desirable business. That's why a buyer is smart to be prepared to move quickly and decisively on an opportunity, if the occasion warrants. And a well prepared buyer is in a position to use all of the modern communications technology at his or her disposal to facilitate rapid and effective communication.

CHAPTER FOUR

HOW A BROKER OR AGENT CAN HELP

One of my favorite business broker stories concerns an engineer, recently laid off his job, who was looking for a business to buy. He happened to tell a broker he'd always wanted to own a hardware store just like the one in the town where he lived.

"I've been bugging the owner to sell to me," the engineer said to the broker. "I've gone in there several times – both as a customer and to find out if he's ready to sell. He always tells me to come back in a few weeks. But every time I follow up with him he says he's not ready yet."

"He probably doesn't want to sell," the broker suggested, "but if you're a customer, he's reluctant to come out and say 'no' to you."

"He's up there in age. I think he should sell," the engineer noted.

"Well I'll be glad to talk to him," the broker suggested.

"You can try," the engineer said. "But I doubt you'll get anywhere."

A week later the broker called the engineer to report he had a contract with the hardware store owner, authorizing the broker to find a buyer. After a few days of negotiations, the parties reached an agreement by which the engineer would buy the hardware store, and the former owner would retire.

"Why didn't you want to sell to me when I asked you?" the buyer asked the outgoing owner. "Now, with the broker involved, you have to pay a commission."

"I'm sorry," the older man said. "I just didn't know how to answer you. I wanted to tell you I was ready to sell, but I didn't know how to go about it – the ins and outs of selling. Then I talked to the broker, he said he could handle everything – that I didn't have to worry about how to sell to you."

What this points out, I think, is that there is a legitimate and a vital role that business brokers can play in bringing about a deal.

Business brokers may not be universally appreciated. Not all are professional. Like people in other fields, not every one is capable and pleasant to deal with. But in most cases, brokers and agents earn their fee by applying their knowledge and skill to the tasks of matching up a buyer and seller, helping them work out their differences and bringing about a closed deal.

What Brokers do for Sellers

For sellers, the work of a broker and/or agent can include about two dozen separate tasks. They include:

1. Provide advice and assistance in preparing the business for sale. The representative might act something like a personal coach in helping and encouraging the seller to carry out the preparation assignments noted in an earlier chapter.

2. Furnish market intelligence, which can be very valuable when determining how to package and present a business in a way that insures a welcome reception when it goes on the market.

3. Offer experienced counsel in establishing an asking price high enough for the seller to get maximum value, but not so high that it discourages interest in the offering.

4. Aid in structuring a business offer that is attractive to a purchaser without derailing the seller's tax planning, or otherwise harming the seller's interests.

5. Suggest ways to find financing so as to increase the appeal and marketability of the business. Some of these financing techniques can be built into the structure of the offering.

6. Create a marketing plan and produce the materials that will be used to offer the business for sale. This requires a special set of skills borrowed from the world of advertising.

7. Expose the business offering to a current and active database of pre-qualified buyers. Sometimes this procedure can result in a sale in a few days.

8. Promote the business for sale in an intelligent and aggressive manner to a general population of buyers so the offering receives wide, controlled exposure. The "controlled" aspect is designed to satisfy a seller's concerns about confidentiality. A variety of promotion outlets may be used, including *www.USABizMart.com*

9. Enlist a network of business brokers and agents to aid in finding a buyer, using informal systems as well as more formal measures, such as an inter-broker business listing service.

10. Gather and analyze market feedback and use it to adjust the structure of the offering if that will improve marketability. A great deal of experience, sound judgment and creativity are needed in this process.

11. Contribute experience and know-how to help in the difficult task of maintaining confidentiality.

12. Interview buyer candidates to make sure they are qualified and have agreed in writing to the seller's requests regarding confidentiality. Eliminate those candidates who don't meet the criteria.

13. Introduce qualified, interested buyers to the business.

14. Conduct follow-up with prospective buyers to determine who is truly interested in the offering.

15. Solicit offers to purchase the business – a job requiring considerable sales talent.

16. Utilize creative persistence and patience for the challenging task of orchestrating negotiations.

17. Manage the due diligence process to make sure it is quickly and satisfactorily completed.

18. Help to answer questions and resolve issues that surface during the period before closing.

19. Contribute the energy and skillful diplomacy sometimes required to keep the deal moving forward through difficulties and over obstacles.

20. Provide the seller with ongoing consultation, advice and reassurance throughout the difficult periods in a sale.

21. Maintain a marketing effort so there are back-up offers. This important process allows a seller to have alternatives if the buyer does not perform, and keeps the buyer motivated to complete the purchase.

22. Use experience and knowledge to make sure seller is not unnecessarily exposed to the many risks that can be inherent in a business transaction.

23. Supervise the completion of the transaction to make sure everything is done correctly and seller's interests are protected.

24. Help seller with any post-sale matters.

Suppose you have read and thought about this list of the two dozen responsibilities of a business broker or agent toward a seller client, and you feel these are duties you can handle in selling your business. Indeed, there are a number of reasons some sellers prefer to self-represent. There are those who feel no one can do a job as well as they can. Then there are sellers so worried about a possible breach of confidence that they want to be involved every time someone is told about their offering.

However, the three most frequently cited reasons for a seller to reject the assistance of the business brokerage community are: the fee, the fee and the fee.

And it is not surprising that a business owner who's had to watch every penny in order to be successful thinks twice, and three times, about engaging the services of a representative in the sale of the business. It means giving up a chunk of the sales proceeds, usually in the range of 10% to 12% of the final selling price.

Some sellers think they can get a bargain by listing with a broker who's accustomed to real estate transactions but wants to try selling a business. The bargain part of it comes about if the broker charges the standard commission – usually 4% to 6% of the selling price – used in home sales. My experience is that sellers trying to save money this way will most likely learn that "you get what you pay for." And that's in the best case!

Why a Seller May Want to Engage a Broker

This job is not for you, however, if you don't feel you have the skills – or the time – to act as your own representative and run your business too.

Besides, you may not be well-served if you attempt to perform the function of a dispassionate third-party. You have a substantial personal stake in the outcome of this campaign. It will be difficult for you to maintain the objectivity needed in all phases of the process of selling your business. That applies especially when you get to the part where the price and terms are being hammered out.

Using a third party is also beneficial in cases where there are deficiencies in your offering, but because it is your business, no one wants to volunteer their criticism or advice. They don't want to hurt your feelings. A disinterested representative is much more likely than you are to learn how your business offering is received by the market. And what your representative finds out can be vital intelligence that you need in order to ultimately find a qualified buyer and close a deal.

If you are in a quandary as to whether you want to engage the services of a representative – you don't want to do the work, but you also don't want to give up a commission – you should know that a professional in the business opportunities field is likely to get a higher price for your business than you will. That's because he or she will be in touch with many more buyers than you. The more prospective purchasers for your business, the greater the chance of getting the requested price. Besides, many brokers and agents have exceptional selling skills they can use to determine the top dollar likely to be paid for your business, and then persuade an interested buyer to agree to that figure.

And, just as your experience in your business has taught you to anticipate and prevent problems, and find solutions when the problems aren't prevented, seasoned business brokers and agents can come to the rescue if you encounter difficulties in the sale of your business that you don't know how to solve. In many cases brokers are able to put things back on track when it appears a deal is headed for failure.

One frequent problem that most skilled brokers can deal with is the buyers' remorse or second thoughts issue that afflicts a number of transactions if they drag on slowly, over a period of several weeks. Brokers are familiar with the pace of a healthy deal and usually are able to keep that pace going, even when questions or problems appear during negotiations, or while parties are engaged in the due diligence process.

Something else to think about, if you're debating benefits vs. costs of engaging a representative to help sell your small business, is the matter of your protection. Even the most experienced business people can be vulnerable to the risk of getting entangled with one of the many difficult situations that can ruin a sale, disrupt the marketing of your business or expose you to unnecessary liabilities. A skilled business broker knows what to watch out for, and can usually steer you clear of legal and other hazards as the business is placed on the market and taken through the complete cycle to a closed escrow.

How Business Brokers and Agents Help a Buyer

A lot of buyers think it's a "no-brainer" to find a good business and then complete a purchase. I've had people tell me that you don't need a broker or agent at all. You just need some common sense and the willingness to work at it a little. And then the rest is easy.

But I think it's important to remember that a competent and experienced broker has a great deal of knowledge about procedure and law that almost no lay person could have. Most buyers don't have a clue about everything they need to do, and need to understand, when they're trying to buy, even a simple, low cost enterprise.

And then what about the expertise that business brokers and agents develop over their months – and years – of working with buyers and sellers, landlords, lenders, franchisors and governmental agencies? That's important know-how that you aren't likely to just figure out or pick up by looking in a book or talking to someone who's bought a business.

Most important are the resources business brokers and agents have at their disposal for use in helping buyers. Business sales professionals have immediate access to listings of businesses for sale, and the information about them, through their brokerages. Their other valuable resources can include lenders (if extra cash is needed to close escrow), inventory services that are quick and reasonable in their rates, business valuation professionals who know the market and understand how it influences value, equipment appraisers, and escrow holders who have special expertise with particular kinds of transactions.

Knowledgeable business sales professionals have all this and more in their phone directories. And I know of instances when a call to the right one of these resources has helped to save a deal that was at risk of going "belly up."

Most buyers are well served by competent representation from the brokerage community. This support can start when someone is first contemplating the idea of buying a company, and needs a way to understand and to work with the market. Then it can extend all the way through the close of a transaction, and beyond.

Despite these reasons, there are some of you in the community of buyers for small businesses who insist you'd rather do it yourself. Perhaps you're imbued with the spirit that fills many entrepreneurs, and results in the habit of independent thinking and extreme self sufficiency. If this is you, my question is: Why not do both?

Go ahead and continue looking for just what you want, talking to owners and sellers, and evaluating the available offerings, while relying on your own resources and business experience to back you up. Meanwhile, interview some brokers and get an idea if there is anyone in the field who can be of assistance.

In fact, you might want to be aware of some of the little-known ways that you can benefit from a good relationship with a business broker or agent. One way is to have access to offerings that aren't generally known about in the marketplace.

Pocket listing

The "pocket listing," for example, is the authority a business sales professional has obtained to offer a business for sale, but is not actively promoting. The seller's intense concerns for confidentiality may be the reason that the offering isn't advertised or made available to other brokers. Perhaps that business is exactly what you've been looking for.

And if the broker with whom you're working can't offer an interesting business proposition to consider, you might want to give him or her an order to fill. Just describe your ideal business in as much detail as possible and the broker can try and match that request by conducting research in the business directories covering your target area.

The broker's strategy is to approach owners of the companies that might meet your criteria, with an explanation that is expressed something like this: "I have a client (that's you) who would be interested in purchasing your business." As you might guess, the brokers are rebuffed in most cases. And in some situations they can't even get access to the owner to have that conversation. Indeed, this soliciting activity can entail a lot of work.

But many brokers are skilled at this procedure, with various strategies for getting the owner's attention and – once that attention is obtained – for getting the person to talk with some candor.

And the brokers know their statistics. Small businesses change hands, on average, every five years. That means that each approach to an owner has one chance in five of turning up a positive. Or put another way, if a broker can approach 20 owners about the idea of selling, the odds dictate that four of them either have their business on the market or are planning to do so.

This campaign, presumably on your behalf, is an effective way for a broker to obtain a listing – the written authorization from a business owner to offer the business for sale at specified price and terms, with the understanding that the owner will pay a commission (the amount or percentage is specified) to the broker upon a successful sale.

Other Arrangements with a Broker or Agent

A business owner who may be thinking about selling, but is not yet fully committed to the process, might still be willing to have a broker try to effect a match with a specific individual whom the broker feels would be an interested and qualified buyer. The result would be an arrangement between broker and seller called a "One-party" listing. It authorizes the broker to introduce the business to the individual named in the listing, and if the buyer agrees to the seller's price and terms, or if the two are able – usually with the broker's help – to come to an agreement, the broker will manage the deal. Upon a successful close, the broker or agent gets a commission from the seller for the amount or percentage specified in the listing.

Many brokers don't care to enter into such an agreement, preferring to work out a full campaign for a seller who is properly preparing the business for sale. That's more likely to result in a deal for a broker than a one-party listing.

But in some cases, the one-party listing is a solution which gives the owner the feeling of maintaining control over the marketing of the business, gives the broker an opportunity to put a deal together, and gives you – if you are the person named in the one-party listing – an opportunity to buy a company that meets your needs, without having to compete with other buyers.

If this approach seems too imprecise for your taste, you can hire a broker to solicit the owner of a specific business you have in mind. You'd be the party in contract with the broker, promising to pay a commission – in this case a finder's fee – in the event you are successful in purchasing the specified company.

Broker to pre-screen offerings

Another way to use your broker is to get him or her to help with the analysis of businesses that have been brought to you for consideration. One complaint about some brokers and agents is that they present companies for sale that have serious defects – such as short-term lease, priced too high, unattractive sales terms, declining industry – without apology or explanation. A serious buyer, after being invited to look at some of these as possible acquisitions, might conclude: "If that's the best this so-called professional can offer, I'm better off without a broker; certainly without this one."

The solution, of course, is to tell the broker to do some preparatory analysis of any business before it's brought to you. If he or she knows you become impatient with offerings that don't make sense, you'll be presented with fewer listings to consider, with less of your time wasted. And when you are introduced to a business offering, it will have passed at least initial scrutiny.

I know buyers who expect their brokers to run an ROI (return on investment) analysis, cash flow projection, market survey and risk assessment on any business possibility brought to them for consideration. This not only reduces the volume of time-wasting offerings for you to see, it also saves you the time and trouble of conducting your own initial research on an offering.

Beware, however, of the danger that a really good business for sale may get connected with another buyer before your broker has had a chance to do the work needed to bring it to you. You may lose a suitable acquisition candidate this way. And you'd better check the broker's work from time to time, to make sure the material you are presented is accurate and complete.

The smart business buyer, then, usually sees advantages in letting business brokers and agents do one of the things they do best – find and present business opportunities for sale – for the benefit of their clients.

You'll do well, in fact, to work with a few brokers – perhaps three or four – so that you'll gain exposure to more listings. Unlike the housing market where every listing is typically available for anyone in the system to sell, the business brokerage field is quite fragmented. Professionals within one brokerage sell only their company's listings and decline to share the listings with other brokerages. This is not a universally popular way of doing things, and you may wonder if a brokerage really represents the best interests of its seller clients when it declines to share its listings with other firms.

Whether this practice is right or wrong, it remains a fact of life in the business. And for a buyer it means your best strategy is to work with more than one brokerage, so as to be exposed to more listings. There may be more time spent initially while you interview, qualify and then select your representatives. But this investment will likely pay off as you'll then have the brokers notifying you of any opportunities they know about which might meet your requirements. This is an efficient way to work, provided you have selected capable brokers and/or agents.

Pay to complete

Some buyers believe in using a third party to help with negotiations. If you've found a business worth buying, and it was through your own efforts, you and the seller can look forward to closing your deal without having a portion of the sales price going to a broker for creating the match-up (of you and the seller). But that assumes you'll be able to make a deal and work out all the details so you can take over the company. What if you can't? It's that worry which motivates some buyers to hire a broker who'll be responsible to handle negotiations and follow up an accepted offer with all the tasks necessary to manage the agreement to a completed deal.

Attorneys also offer this service, but may not have the skills at the ready as would an experienced broker who's accustomed to negotiating the sale of small businesses with regularity. The deal to strike is that the broker only gets paid – and usually it would be a flat fee – if he or she is successful in getting you and the seller to agree on terms of a purchase, and then is able to manage the transaction until it closes.

Conclusion

While there are a few business brokers and agents who lack competence and integrity, just as there are a handful of participants in any profession who should be avoided, the majority of business sales professionals can provide a lot of information, as well as expertise, to help clients achieve their goals of buying and/or selling small businesses. With at least 24 ways that they can help sellers, business sales professionals can be valuable resources for business owners wanting to sell. Included in their strengths are the ability to act as the disinterested third party and to bring a fresh perspective to, say, stalled negotiations. And brokers and agents offer a vital function for buyers by educating them about market realities, not to mention informing buyers about suitable candidates the broker or agent can call up from the base of current listings to which he or she has access.

KEY POINTS FROM THIS CHAPTER

❖ *Look at the 24 tasks that brokers can provide for their seller clients. If you can manage these responsibilities – some of them can be difficult – perhaps you don't need help from a broker.*

❖ *What a capable business sales professional can bring to a seller is experience, the benefit of that third party perspective and, of course, the market of qualified buyers, one of whom might be suitable as a new owner of the business.*

❖ *It's not surprising that a business owner who has had to watch every penny to build a successful small business is reluctant to part with 10% or 12% of the sales price for a commission when that owner doesn't feel there is much value a broker will bring to the deal.*

❖ *Working with a broker who specializes in home sales, not businesses, because of the lower commission requirement may seem like a smart strategy, but you usually "get what you pay for." This has been the lesson for several business owners who didn't get the results they wanted because of poor business representation.*

❖ *Problems such as buyer's remorse, for example, are dealt with frequently by skilled business brokers. They may be better equipped to handle such difficulties in your transaction than you are, which is a good reason for having one represent you.*

❖ *For the business buyer, brokers offer access to dozens, maybe hundreds of business offerings, along with the help in analyzing these opportunities.*

❖ *A "pocket listing" may represent an opportunity for a business buyer to get access to an appealing offering before others learn about it. The secret to finding out about these situations is to have a particularly good rapport with a business broker or agent.*

❖ *If a broker is willing to take a one-party listing, it may represent an opportunity for an owner to sell without going to a lot of trouble in preparing the business for sale. There is no commission due if a sale is not made to the person named in the listing.*

❖ *For a buyer, the one-party listing that names the buyer is a way of getting possible access to a business which has not been made available to all buyers.*

❖ *A buyer can "train" the broker to bring only qualified listings to the buyer's attention. Much time will be saved by not looking at unsuitable candidates. It's also possible, however, that a great opportunity will not become known by a qualified buyer, because it was sold before the broker had a chance to prescreen the offering.*

❖ *Buyers are advised to work with three or four brokers, so as to benefit from the broadened exposure and increased chances of finding the right business.*

❖ *There's no reason a seller or a buyer cannot hire an experienced business sales professional to help complete a deal. The fee would be less than a sales commission, and would be paid in return for specific services, such as performing the duties of negotiator or giving advice on handling difficult aspects of a transaction.*

CHAPTER FIVE

SELECTING AND WORKING WITH A BROKER OR AGENT

Okay. You understand that it might make sense to work with a business broker or agent to help you sell your business, or to help you find a suitable company to purchase.

Qualities to Look For in a Representative

But how does one select a representative? There are a number of professionals in the business who are committed to a high level of customer service and honest dealing. But the business also attracts individuals who are drawn to the action – the wheeling and dealing aspect of the business – and who see inexperienced buyers and sellers as potential targets for their questionable techniques. Is there a way to be sure of choosing someone who will truly help you?

Interested in helping you achieve your objectives

In most cases a broker or agent earns a commission by selling a business – the money coming from the seller's proceeds. And in most states, the business sales professional is considered an agent of the seller. What these facts suggest is that any work a broker or agent does for you, if you're the buyer, is performed only in the hopes of selling you a business and collecting a commission from the business' seller.

Is this why some buyers have a hard time trusting business brokers?

And yet as a practical matter most brokers and agents are able to work effectively with buyers, are able to focus on the needs of those "clients," can earn their trust, argue on their behalf during negotiations, and make sure the buyer is protected all the way through the completion of a transaction.

That's the kind of broker you want. So it's important that anyone wishing to sell a business to you begins this process by asking what you want, and then listening to the answer.

You should be able to discern rather quickly whether the broker you are interviewing is paying attention to your explanation of what you want, or is simply nodding the head and waiting for you to finish talking so you can listen to what he or she wants to tell you about the brokerage's latest listings.

Do the offerings presented to you reflect the criteria you've outlined or is the broker just offering you whatever they're trying to sell? Do you have to point out the deficiencies in proposed businesses or does the broker say something akin to: "I'm not going to tell you about the distribution company because the asking price is much too high?" Does the broker ask more questions about your interests to clearly understand, in detail, your criteria?

Notice how much interest the broker has in your requirements and how much attention is paid to your questions and comments. It's an important clue as to whether the broker or agent is interested in really representing you.

If you're not convinced the person's foremost objective is to determine exactly what you want and then try and get if for you, it's best to strike him or her from your list and work with somebody else.

And sellers who select a broker or agent based on this requirement can leave much of the marketing work to the representative, knowing that tasks such as maintaining confidentiality of the offering will be managed with competency and care. The broker may have some ideas to help you get the business sold quickly and at the price and terms that work for you. But if he or she wants to tell you how the company will be packaged and marketed before you've had a chance to explain what you need, this may not be a representative with your best interests at heart.

Tells you the truth

It is not in your interests, however, to have a representative who tells you just what you want to hear. Whether you're buying or selling, you need hard and accurate information about the characteristics of the market and the chances of meeting your objectives. Remember that the broker or agent who is in the habit of putting a "spin" on the facts, not only puts you at a disadvantage if you act on incomplete or misleading data, but also may put you at risk of legal consequences if there were misrepresentations made about your participation when a deal was put together. It's possible for you, the buyer, to get sued by a seller if your agent made false promises that you were going to perform a certain way, such as signing papers or putting more money into a deal, even if you had no intention of doing so.

Ask yourself if the individual who wants to represent you seems to be straightforward and realistic. Does he or she give you the bad news and the disappointing facts along with the broker's standard messages of hopeful optimism? Whether you are buying or selling, if your representative does not consistently tell it "like it is" you may pay the consequences by passing on a good deal because you were persuaded to wait for something better. Or you may enter into a transaction on terms that aren't as favorable as you might have achieved, had you known all the straight facts. And what's worse, as mentioned above, if the broker's exaggerations about your capabilities or your intent causes harm to another party, you may well find yourself in court at the defendant's table.

Has expertise and experience

The ideal way for a seller or a buyer to be served by a business sales professional, falls between extremes of dictating to you how your needs should be addressed (without listening carefully and considering your position), and assuring you that whatever you want can be achieved. While understanding what you want and trying to satisfy that, your broker should talk things over with you, telling you if he or she thinks you are unrealistic about your expectations and letting you in on facts or information you may not have.

Whenever you make an offer to purchase a business, you'll want the broker to have some skill at presenting your position forcefully, and the ability to press for the things that are important to you. You won't be present during all the negotiations taking place between the seller and the brokers involved, so don't you want to be confident that the person representing you is arguing persuasively on your behalf? And if your representative has some experience, he or she will be able to cite the facts to prove that you are a strong buyer and that your offer might represent the seller's best deal.

If you're considering brokers from the seller's side of the equation, you're likely to want the representative who negotiates on your behalf, to apply knowledge, experience and selling skill; to present your case in a way that is forceful and convincing.

You also want your broker to have some skills at business analysis. Even though I know a great deal about analyzing a set of business records, and about evaluating how a company may perform in the future – based on its infrastructure and the marketplace in which it functions – I still find it valuable to get the feedback from other brokers, to learn if they have a different way of assessing a particular business offering.

You may enjoy an important added benefit if your representative's expertise includes the ability to bring creative solutions to problems that crop up either during negotiations or while trying to close a transaction. It's not uncommon for a deal to stall on any number of issues, misunderstandings and uncompleted tasks. And that's when skilled brokers and agents really earn their money. They find ways, for example, to get parties in agreement over a contentious matter, to work out compromises with landlords and lenders, and to satisfy requirements of governmental agencies without damaging the elements of a transaction.

And while you're questioning a broker or agent candidate about his or her experience and expertise, ask for some examples of how the person was able to keep a transaction moving forward to a successful conclusion. A number of deals seem to die at some point between the accepted offer and the closing. If your representative can maintain the momentum, once you're in contract to sell your business or to buy the company you want, that talent may make the difference between the achievement of your objectives, and the wasting of your time in the marketplace for small businesses.

Knows the business

Along with experience, a competent broker gains the important knowledge about business sales that is needed from the day you launch your campaign as a seller or buyer, to the moment you add your final signature representing the achievement of your objective. Knowing the laws governing business transactions is a must. The representative you choose also should understand how the laws are applied in a variety of situations.

Added to this knowledge, the capable business sales professional, needs to be familiar with customs and practices in your area. What constitutes an enforceable contract? Does your agreement meet the legal definition and the community's accepted standards? If not – if the broker didn't construct your deal correctly – the person who has signed documents to buy your business may be able to get out of the agreement if something more interesting comes along.

Are there closing requirements that must be followed in a particular order for the transaction to be completed? If the final stages of a transaction are not orchestrated correctly, you may find the process dragging on for weeks or months, rather than days. The broker will claim it's the fault of the bank, the franchisor or the state's alcohol beverage control agency. In fact, the inadequate planning and inept handling of closing procedures may be the problem. And the longer your deal continues to languish in that gray area, uncompleted, the greater the chances that it will self destruct.

A solid, working knowledge of the details needed to successfully sell your business: That's what your representative must have – or must be able to access, quickly and whenever needed – at his or her company.

And if you're planning to purchase a company, make sure the important knowledge about the industry and the particulars of deal-making, are part of what your representative will bring to the process.

Resources

Talent, experience and knowledge are key attributes to look for in the broker who will help you successfully sell your business, or lead you to the company of your dreams. And these abilities should be grounded with the resources that enable brokers to access buyers and business offerings, get the word out about your requirements, and locate the services – such as lending and escrow support – that will make it possible for you to realize your business goals.

Is the prospective broker a member of a multiple listing network? Does he or she have access to a number of businesses for sale? Does the professional use online services such as *www.USABizMart.com* to make sure a listing receives the widest exposure possible, and to circulate a buyer's requirements?

Find out if the prospective representative has relationships with escrow companies, business appraisers, equipment valuation services, inventory services and small business lenders. You'd like to learn, when interviewing prospective brokers, not only what they know, but also who they know and on whom they can call to help in the campaign to achieve your objectives.

Rapport

Think of your business broker as a member of your team. And consider that accomplishing most anything is easier with teamwork.

Certainly that's true in the case of a project as difficult as matching a qualified buyer and a suitable small business, negotiating an agreement acceptable to all parties, helping the buyer through his or her examination of the business, and the seller with verification of the ability of the buyer, making sure the releases, agreements, permits and approvals necessary to complete the transition are in place, then handling all final details so the deal can be successfully closed.

To achieve your business goals in a reasonable period of time at terms that work for you may not require that you and your broker work together with the precision of a super bowl-winning quarterback and his favorite receiver. Or a brain surgeon and chief surgical assistant. But if there's poor communication and a lack of understanding between the two of you, the task will be much more difficult, if not impossible.

It's critical that your broker clearly understands your needs and priorities and it's important that you know what to realistically expect your broker or agent to be able to do. In the heat of negotiations, or during the difficult periods of due diligence, it's easy to let emotion influence reason. Even the calmest, most logical principals in a deal can find themselves frustrated when things don't move according to plan. That's when it's particularly important that you and your broker have a person-to-person connection that allows you to work through tough problems so you can achieve your final goal.

But you can't approach this need with objective solutions, as you would when asking a broker-candidate about years of experience, and requesting a list of references. The question of rapport needs to be answered by you, using more subjective analysis.

Are you able to communicate with this person? Does he or she understand your problems? Does the broker or agent candidate clearly express himself or herself about the challenges you will face and do you get the impression the person is prepared for those challenges?

These are some of the more subtle of the factors that go into choosing a business broker to work with. They're not easy to quantify or describe objectively. And yet, how you "feel" about your business broker can greatly influence your ability to work together. It's also a predictor of your likelihood for success.

Is it Worth the Fee?

If you're a seller, interviewing business brokers and agents, you'll learn that their fees are usually a percentage of your selling price, typically between 10 and 12. There may be a minimum fee for transactions with low selling prices. And if the size of your business warrants a price in excess of $1 million, a business broker may determine the commission using a formula with a sliding scale tied to final selling price.

Only you can decide if it is worth the fee to have a representative help you in the sale. Be sure to consider all the factors and conduct a full cost/benefit analysis. That should include trying to anticipate the time and skill required, the risks involved and the possibility that a business broker – with experience and a database of prospective buyers – will be able to sell for a higher price than you will.

Verify with References

How does the seller or the buyer know, for sure, the depth of experience or extent of knowledge possessed by a candidate for the job of his or her business broker?

That's why it's vital to get a list of clients, at least five – ten is better, for whom the broker or agent has worked.

Ask for names and contact information. Then be sure to call or email every one of them. Don't stop at the two who head the list. Anyone can find two people to brag about his honesty and business expertise. Communicate with every reference; ask if there were problems with their deals and whether the business sales professional was able to handle those difficulties. Was the person easy to work with? Was he or she able to keep the transaction moving toward completion, or did it stall because of unanticipated complications, misunderstandings and uncompleted tasks? Did the broker convey an attitude of competence? Were there any post-sale complaints?

Ask the contact whether any stumbling blocks or delays in their transaction were the result of broker inattention. And ask if the person would hire that same broker again, and whether they'd recommend that others do the same.

And be sure to find out when the reference and the broker were involved together in a business transaction. The more recent the better. I'm usually leery of references that are more than three or four years old.

Most people feel that the willingness to submit a list of references is somehow proof of ability. "Surely she wouldn't give me these references if they aren't good," the reasoning goes.

But brokers have been known to provide a list of people in response to the request and then hope and assume – in many cases correctly – that the references will never be contacted.

If, in checking your prospective broker's list of references, you find his gardener, a next door neighbor, and a couple of business owners who never had success working with him, it's best to assume that the broker never expected you to actually contact the names on the list. You can also conclude that the broker does not qualify to handle your business.

Assuming, though, that your prospective broker(s) comes well recommended by people who relied on the person to buy or sell a business, that's the confirmation you need to let you know this might be the right professional to help you in your sale or purchase of a business.

How Buyers Can Work with Your Representative(s)

For that broker or agent to help you achieve success, however, it's necessary that you're an effective partner – that you work well with the professional, or with the professionals (if you're a buyer wanting broad representation) you've selected to represent you.

And working well with your professional partner begins with the simple practice of being straightforward.

You may have heard the following: "It's better not to let a broker know how much money you have. If you do, they're always trying to get you to use it all."

This is a rather common opinion stated by buyers. And my reaction is this: If you don't trust your broker, you need to either get a new one, or you need to adjust your ideas about how to work with someone who's trying to help you find a good business. Your broker or agent can't do a good job for you if he or she is not armed with all the relevant information about what you want and what you can do.

I remember being scolded by a client – a man who was looking for a non-retail business – because I didn't tell him about a convenience store located in his neighborhood that had come on the market.

He agreed that the business was well outside the parameters he had given me; then said: "But I would have made an exception in this case."

Until brokers and agents develop the ability to read the minds of their clients, it's better for you, the buyer, to give your representative complete information about what you want, so that you don't miss an opportunity.

What business would you most like to buy? What is your second choice? Are there other types of enterprises you would consider if the circumstances were ideal? These are some of the questions to answer for yourself, and then discuss with the representative helping you to find a business. Also in the category of your requirements are topics such as how much money you need to earn and how many hours you want to work every week.

Your representative also needs to know, in as much detail as you can provide, about your capabilities: The sum of cash you have for a down payment and working capital, your tolerance for risk, your experience and skills, the level of debt you are willing to take on, the value of your real and personal property and the extent to which you are prepared to use it to collateralize any obligations you take on as part of a purchase.

Equipped with a good understanding about you as a potential buyer, the business sales professional will be able to help you and even will be motivated to work on your behalf. That's the payoff to you for being open and honest with your broker, and for providing all the information needed to serve you properly.

And a word of caution that buyers who aren't certain what they want in terms of the type of business, who aren't specific about the amount of cash they've got set aside for this purpose, and don't know – or won't reveal – how much real or personal property they're willing to put up as collateral in the event of seller financing, won't get a lot of broker attention. Business sales professionals have more than enough customers to stay busy. And so their focus will always remain with those buyers who show they are serious and committed by furnishing ample information about what they're looking for and what they can handle.

Good Broker Communication Imperative for Sellers

One colleague tells the story of a woman who engaged the services of a business broker specifically known for his experience in the beauty services industry so she could sell her hair salon and retire. Although the seller found it a bit difficult to deal with him, she was impressed with the glowing recommendations from the referrals she checked and with his experience. In fact, the broker came to the salon a day after the listing was taken, bringing a buyer who owned other, similar businesses.

The prospective buyer proceeded to fire off a series of questions that the seller was unable to answer. Curiously, he didn't care to learn about her customers, the equipment, or the other dynamics that the seller considered important to the business. This buyer was apparently interested only in the financials. And the things he was investigating – "dollars per chair" and "profit per employee" – were principles she hadn't studied, though she'd run the shop successfully for over 20 years.

Not only did the seller not see that buyer again, she didn't hear much from the broker after that. She eventually learned that the broker considered her "difficult to deal with," apparently because she didn't have the kinds of analyses at her fingertips that he required.

After expiration of the six month listing with that broker, the seller again interviewed brokers, this time choosing a less experienced professional, but one with whom she could easily communicate. Eventually the business was sold, but it took longer than the seller had anticipated.

The story points out the importance of a good understanding between seller and broker, and the fact that the seller didn't do a very good job of learning what would be required of her. She didn't insist on feedback from the marketing campaign, and she failed to push her representative to make a real sales effort on behalf of her business. The broker was at fault as well. But it was the seller who suffered the impact of their poor relationship and she realized later, when talking to the new broker, that she should have been more proactive with the original representative.

To work effectively with the broker helping you sell, it is imperative that you can communicate with one another. Make sure the professional representing you will be in touch with you at least two or three times a week. In fact, you can have that provision written right into the listing agreement.

Have the broker put in writing how frequently you can expect to receive an update on the marketing efforts – who has been introduced to your business, what the reaction was and so forth. You even can ask that the broker specify the dollar figure that will be spent to promote and advertise your business for sale. (A budget of $2,000 or so is not unreasonable). Covering these points in the listing agreement helps to set the tone for the seller/broker relationship. And if there is a good relationship, with plenty of communication and realistic expectations on both sides, you stand a better chance of accomplishing the sale of your business at a satisfactory price and terms.

It's not critical that the broker specializes in your type of business, but it is important that he or she is willing to work hard to make sure your business is exposed to many potential buyers. And while some sellers are impressed if a representative brags about having a large "stable" of listings – as if every business person in town wants their help – I think you're better off dealing with someone who has a half dozen listings. With a manageable inventory, your broker will have the time to give you the service your business needs, so it can be marketed properly and sold in a reasonable period of time.

And be careful to avoid so-called "listings" that require a fee to be paid at the beginning. If there is no value provided, except for the broker's claim that he or she will do their best to find you a buyer, you'll soon meet with a big disappointment – perhaps an expensive one. If you're going to pay for services, make sure you receive something you can use, such as a package that promotes your business in an appealing way, or an appraisal conducted by a trained small business valuation expert to establish what your business is worth.

It's fair to ask a prospective broker to limit the length of your exclusive agreement to three months or six months. If you feel the person and their brokerage are doing a good job for you, but the listing expires before a sale is achieved, you can always agree to an extension. This puts you in a stronger position and is preferable to getting locked into a longer Exclusive Right contract (such as 9-month or 12-month listing) with someone who feels they have plenty of time and doesn't quite get around to selling your business.

It is not fair, however, to keep important information from your broker. Your business is not expected to be perfect. It may have deficiencies in, for example, the length of the lease, the dependence on a small number of major customers, or the deteriorating condition of your equipment. It's important that you level with the professionals representing you. Don't surprise them. Let them help you by disclosing to them all of the aspects of your offering that may be a problem in finding a buyer.

Keeping secrets from, and springing unexpected facts on your broker or agent merely interrupts the selling momentum and disrupts your relationship. And those are the kinds of problems that interfere with a successful sale of your business.

Some Alternative Arrangements for Sellers

What if you have a buyer, someone who is already interested in owning your business and you'd like some help putting the deal together? Or suppose you currently have the business listed and you are approached by a buyer, independently of your representative. And how should you handle this situation: A buyer is introduced during a listing, the listing expires and the buyer returns without the broker, wanting to deal with you individually – suggesting that since the broker is no longer involved, the price can be lower? And is there a way to get two different brokers working for you if you like them both and don't want to choose one to the exclusion of the other?

These and a number of other, similarly perplexing situations, are rather common occurrences in the market for small businesses. You, a seller, should be aware of different arrangements with brokers and agents that can help deal with these scenarios.

Pay for project

The owner of an air conditioning service company wants to retire and has made an agreement with an employee to buy the business. Is it necessary to have a complicated arrangement with a broker? If you have the buyer and the agreed-on price and terms, you need only ask a competent professional – a broker or an attorney (the later will be more expensive) – to draft the buy/sell agreement and help you work out the details needed to close the deal. Have prospective representative give you a quote, and work with the professional who seems competent, but charges the least.

The listing agreement

But you may need to enter into a listing agreement if you'll need help finding a buyer and working out a deal. For starters, it would be useful to review the basic characteristics of a listing agreement – the employment contract used in most states to define the agency relationship between the broker and business seller. Just like a listing agreement on a house, this is the promise of the broker to market the subject property – in this case a business opportunity – for sale, to show and provide information about the property for the benefit of prospective buyers, to solicit offers, aid in negotiations between buyer and seller, and work to secure a ratified transaction (a deal that's signed by both buyer and seller). The cost of this work, including advertising fees and incidental expenses, is paid by the broker. In return for this promise, the seller pledges to pay the broker a commission. The commission amount is always specified in the agreement and usually is expressed as a percentage of the selling price. The commission, also called the fee, is customarily due to be paid upon the broker's successful accomplishment of his or her tasks, when the work culminates in a completed transaction.

The base agreement is called an Exclusive Right to Sell. It commences on the date specified in the contract and terminates at an agreed date in the future – usually three or six months from the beginning date.

Because of the provision about exclusivity in this type of listing, the brokerage in the contract is the only one authorized to represent the seller in this capacity during the life of the agreement and any extensions. And the broker is entitled to a commission if the subject property is sold to anyone during the listing period, whether that buyer is obtained by the broker or not. The agreements almost always specify that if a buyer, introduced to the property while the listing is active, comes back later, after the listing's expiration, the broker is entitled to the commission if a sale to that buyer is achieved within a specified period of time after the introduction took place. For example, if a buyer is introduced by the business broker to a service station in May, and waits till after September (four months later) when the listing expires, to make an offer to purchase the station, the broker still is entitled to a commission if a deal is struck between buyer and seller. This is meant to protect the broker's right to commission if a seller and buyer want to have a deal, and collude to save the commission by postponing their buy/sell contract till after the listing expires.

As you might imagine, it's important for brokers and sellers to keep track of whom they talked to, and when. If there is a dispute under a listing contract, the final determination of rights will probably hinge on the facts of the case. And parties involved will need to prove their version of what happened.

As the Exclusive Right to Sell contract provides brokers the most control and protection, it is the form of agreement used for the majority of listings. And it is the one recommended by most brokers and agents.

But there are other kinds of agreements by which brokers and sellers agree to do business. You should be aware of your options. And you also should be aware that many brokers and agents decline to enter into the non-exclusive listing agreements.

Exclusive Agency

If you select a single broker to represent you, but want the right to sell to your own buyer without an obligation to the broker for a commission, the most appropriate agreement is what is called an Exclusive Agency in most states.

You are not permitted to sign with other brokers, according to this understanding. For you to make the sale without obligation to the broker, remember that you must be able to demonstrate that the buyer is someone you contacted independently, not a person introduced to the business by the broker.

Open listing

Under this looser arrangement, practiced by brokers in virtually every part of the country, the broker is assured of being compensated for a sales commission if, and only if, that broker comes up with the ultimate buyer. It is like a finders' fee. Meanwhile, the seller is free to make his or her own sale and to work with most any other broker without obligation to anyone except the broker who introduced the buyer under an Open listing. One broker's Open listing is automatically cancelled if the seller signs an exclusive with another broker.

One-Party listing

A variation on the Open listing, the One-Party agreement can be used when the seller is not willing to offer the business for sale through the broker in the usual way, but is willing to pay a specified commission to a broker if the one person, mentioned by name on the One-Party listing, purchases the business.

This kind of agreement might come about in the case where a broker approaches a business owner and explains that he has a client interested in purchasing the business. The broker may say he wants to introduce that individual to the business, handle any resulting transaction and receive a commission for a successful sale. In the event the owner's response is: "If this person buys the business for my price, I'll pay you the commission," the result can be a One-party listing between seller and broker, naming that buyer, and specifying the price and terms requested by the seller. If a seller agrees to a listing like this, it's a good idea to include an expiration date.

Conclusion

Common sense is a good guideline when determining how to select a broker or an agent to represent you in selling or purchasing a small business. Clearly the person should be competent, experienced, and have good references, which you check to make sure the person is being straightforward with you. It also is important, for this to be a successful relationship, that you do your part to be straightforward, communicative and easy to deal with.

Buyers probably want to work with a few representatives, and it's important to stay in touch with those brokers and agents so they know you are serious and still in the market. Sellers are advised that there are different arrangements possible with brokers to represent you. But whether you have one representative through an Exclusive Right to Sell, or a selection of brokers working with Open listings, you will have a better chance of success in finding a good buyer and closing a deal if you make sure to be honest and straightforward with those who are trying to help you.

KEY POINTS FROM THIS CHAPTER

❖ *The ability to "shut up and listen" is an important quality for a broker who wants to represent the buyer or seller of a small business. Your representative should hear what you want and try to work with you on that basis.*

❖ *And if you go to market, either to sell or to buy, the desirable broker representative will let you know about the realities to be faced. Being honest with you is a key characteristic of the person you want to represent you. Not only do you want him or her to give you information you can act on successfully, you also want to know the broker is not going to put you at risk of getting sued by making statements to others which misrepresent your capabilities and intentions.*

❖ *Experience, competency and knowledge also are important qualities to look for in the broker or agent representative(s) you choose. Additionally, he or she should have, readily available, the resources needed to assist you. That includes access to information about businesses for sale – if you're interested in making a purchase, or a database of qualified buyers to match with the business you wish to place on the market.*

❖ *And don't forget that rapport is vital. A representative who is qualified in other respects may not be much help to you if the two of you cannot communicate well and work together effectively.*

❖ *It's vital that broker candidates give you references – at least five, and ten is better – so that you can verify the ability and reputation of the person who wants to represent you. Make sure to contact those references – every one you can.*

❖ *For a buyer to have a successful relationship with a broker or agent, it's important not only that the agent is able, but also that the buyer does a good job of being straightforward and clear about what is of interest in the market of businesses for sale.*

❖ *A buyer also should inform the broker about his or her professional background, work skills and financial capabilities.*

❖ *And it's a good idea to stay in touch with representatives so they know you're still serious and ready to move on the "right" deal.*

❖ *If you want to sell your business and already have a buyer and an agreement, you should have no trouble finding a competent professional to write up the deal and help you close it, all for a reasonable fee.*

❖ *For sellers, the "dos" of good broker interaction include telling the truth about your situation and the condition of the business, and making a point of staying in touch with the representative. In fact, it doesn't hurt to put into any listing agreement the requirement that the broker contact you on a regular (two or three times per week) basis.*

❖ *It's also a good idea to have the listing agreement reflect the broker's responsibility to advertise your business for sale.*

❖ *One bit of advice for sellers is that you limit listing contracts to three or six months. No need to tie yourself to a longer-term agreement and risk being committed to a broker who does an inadequate job.*

❖ *Another bit of advice is to be aware there are different legal arrangements you can make with a representative in most states. The Exclusive Right to Sell is a vote of confidence by you in the broker, and you'd like the person's best attention and effort.*

❖ *Non exclusive listings that sellers can enter into with brokers in most states work like a finder's fee contract as with the Open listing (I'll pay you if, and only if, you bring the buyer, and I'll retain the right to work with other brokers,) or Exclusive Agency agreements (you'll be my only broker, but I can make a deal to my buyer without owing you anything.)*

❖ *In no case should a buyer or seller contract with a broker in a deal that calls for up-front fees – particularly if there is no real value inherent in the agreement. There are plenty of competent brokers to sell your business or find you a business with the understanding they only get paid if they help you meet your objectives. There's no benefit to working with someone who wants you to pay the fee first, with the representative doing the work second.*

CHAPTER SIX

WHAT'S THE RIGHT PRICE? – NET EARNINGS CALCULATION

Various aspects of the small businesses offered for sale on the market can readily be analyzed, counted, measured and evaluated. We know what equipment the seller is offering, we can determine the value of the inventory and we can calculate the amount of the payments to be made by buyer to seller, given a balance amount, interest rate and payoff period.

When it comes to establishing the right price for the entire business however, we're on less solid ground. Various theories are advanced by different contributors to the discussion about setting the proper amount at which a small business should sell.

In fact, pricing a business for sale can be as much an art as a science. And because there is no single and definitive method for assigning an exact market value to a small business, many sellers feel justified in building plenty of negotiating room into their asking prices, while some buyers make offers that are unrealistic in the other (too low) direction.

The different opinions expressed by buyers and by sellers as to how much money a business should fetch on the open market are influenced by the motivation of each person asked. And what they profess may not correspond to their behavior when they get into the heat of negotiations.

But there are some guidelines that can be followed by the seller establishing a value for a business, and a buyer determining how much to pay. And whether you are working with a broker or on your own, you ought to have a basic idea of the elements that go into pricing a small business. As a seller, you want some notions of business values when talking to brokers or prospective buyers. And if you're looking to purchase a company, you'd like to have a sense as to whether the price asked for it is realistic.

Perhaps these ideas will be helpful.

It's Not Real Estate

While some people think of real estate in the same terms as a business, it's a mistake to use principles involved in the sale of real property to resolve questions pertaining to sale of a business.

If the public had access to a database of actual prices recently paid for small businesses in every area of the country, and if there was some uniformity about small businesses and one accounting method used in each case, perhaps we could rely on the comparables approach to valuation. It works well in the real estate market. The selling price of your neighbor's house is an excellent reference point to use as you determine the value of yours.

But none of these conditions exist. There is no place to look up selling prices of businesses. And no two businesses are alike.

To emphasize this point, an executive employed by a fast food franchisor tells a story about one of the company's franchisees who owned two businesses in a Southern California community. In most every respect, the businesses were identical. They had been built at about the same time for nearly identical costs, and they were located just over a mile apart, in very similar areas, each in a retail strip center surrounded by mid-priced residential development. As the owner was involved in day-to-day operations of both, the management was the same.

And yet one of the businesses averaged a few dollars more in profit most every month over a two year period. It took careful analysis to determine that minor variations in traffic patterns tended to yield slightly higher gross revenues in the more profitable of the two. And the less profitable store had been affected by a series of unexpected problems, such as a power outage that affected the area and a broken sewer line that required businesses on that block to be closed for a couple of days.

These small and subtle differences became big factors when the owner decided to sell. He put each on the market separately and received about $100,000 more for the slightly more profitable business. The executive concludes the example by noting that had the properties been homes, instead of businesses in the area, any small differences between them would have been expressed as a tiny variation in selling price – not the six figure difference that occurred in the case of the sold businesses.

Considering the lack of comparables to aid in valuation of small businesses – the way homes and other real estate properties can be assigned asking prices – how does an owner determine the correct amount to ask for his or her small business, and how does a buyer know the fair and correct amount to pay?

And It's Not a Passive Investment

A seller who makes the mistake of comparing the purchase of her small company to an investment in the stock market – where multiples are several times the figures we'll consider – has forgotten that the typical small business purchaser is buying a career and will work in the business.

An investment in a public company might cost several times annual earnings per share, but most investors are doing nothing to contribute to that value. By contrast, the buyer of a small business is actually earning his or her salary by the work of managing the company, calling on prospective clients, running the equipment, answering the phone, dealing with an unhappy customer and sweeping the floors. As far as the buyer is concerned, every penny received is well earned.

When the purchase price of someone's business is considered from this perspective, a buyer could claim that there is no return on the investment but that the income is entirely a result of the owner's labor. The seller might disagree, and claim that the new owner can hire someone to handle those responsibilities. Under this scenario, of course, the buyer's income from the business will be dramatically reduced by the size of the salary paid to the new employee.

A smart buyer will then point out that he can get the same return by buying common stock in a blue-chip company. He's almost certain to get the anticipated earnings with no work and without the headaches and risks that go with small business ownership.

This very argument between seller and buyer has taken place many times when there was a disagreement about value. It demonstrates how the purchase of a business differs from a passive investment and why intelligent sellers and buyers of small businesses should have an understanding of the realities in the marketplace in order to assign a "fair" price to a company being sold.

Two Reliable Factors that Mirror Reality

The best way to gain a clear marketplace perspective is recommended by experienced business brokers, rejecting complex theoretical approaches in favor of the most common principles they can derive from completed deals. Their idea is to focus on two major dynamics: One, the expectations of a small business buyer; and two, how well a subject business performs in relation to the expectations. And then there are a number of factors which help to adjust the basic value to reflect all the realities of the market and the situation.

The first part of this approach is to understand a typical buyer's expectations regarding purchase of a small business. Remembering that most buyers of small businesses, whether service companies, retail firms, food enterprises and so forth, are seeking to – as one broker puts it – "buy a job," it would be useful to analyze the issue from that perspective.

Calculate ROI (Return on Investment) for Owner/Operator

"How much money do you want to make?" That is usually one of the first questions a business broker or agent will ask of a new buyer client.

And the answer, for most buyers is: "As much as I can and certainly enough to support my family."

Whether that figure is $50,000 per year, or $75,000, or $200,000 or $456,000, the buyer will soon learn that what he or she must pay will be a function of the income desired. And the value of a business tends to form around this central theme. If buyers in a particular area feel that they should get back their investment in say, two years of owning, operating and working in the subject business, then their "right" price will be twice the annual output of cash and cash equivalents that flow to the owner. If they are prepared to wait for three years' work in the business before the investment is recovered, then the business will sell for a multiple of three times annual cash flow.

This principle does, of course, raise a few key questions, that should be addressed as part of this discussion. The questions are: How is the multiple determined? Exactly how does a buyer measure cash flow? And what about the terms of a deal – does the amount of cash required influence the use of a multiple?

Multiple of Earnings

This idea is largely a reflection of supply and demand. In a number of places throughout the U.S., the experience of the past several years demonstrates that people purchasing a means of livelihood, have been willing to go along with an asking a price that exceeds a year's income from that business. But in most cases they have not been willing to pay more than a multiple of three to four times the earnings in the most recent year. And to complete this balance of market forces, most sellers have been in agreement with this formula. The meeting of demand and supply forces at the range of approximately two to three times annual cash flow has established the market rate that has prevailed in many parts of the country through the past few decades.

The multiple, expressed another way, is the expectation of annual adjusted net income from the business, as it relates to the amount of cash that was invested in purchase price and operating capital. In other words, the 2.5 multiple suggests that the buyers want their money back in two-and-a-half years.

The beauty of this solution is that it's not theoretical. It reflects the actual behavior in the market. And its weakness is that it's a general rule of thumb, subject to exceptions and disputes among interested parties.

Some business appraisers believe the price should include inventory, while others consider inventory to be in addition to the price. The right solution for this problem depends on a few factors, including the amount of inventory in relation to the value of other assets

In the give and take of the marketplace, a distribution or manufacturing business – a class of businesses much in demand – might bring a 3.0 or 3.5 multiple. For a business with problems – examples include a short-term lease, aging equipment and market encroachment by competitors – the correct multiple might be closer to 1.0 or 1.5. Retail businesses frequently fetch 2.5 to 3 times the annual adjusted net income if inventory is part of that price. The multiple might be a bit lower if it is not meant to include the inventory needed.

A number of factors go into this equation, of course. And if circumstances were to change substantially, the multiple might change as well. For example, a profound improvement in the local economy might reduce the risk involved in taking over a business, which could have the effect of raising the multiple. If buyers were more certain that they would be successful in their new business, and anticipated a strong likelihood of rapid growth, they might be willing to pay four or more times current annual income as a purchase price.

An example of the reverse effect would be an improvement in the employment conditions in the area. With companies paying high salaries and providing substantial benefits to lure workers, there might be fewer active candidates ready to make a purchase in the small business market. This would likely result in a reduction of the multiple as businesses lowered asking prices in the competition for buyers.

Measuring Cash Flow: Adjusted Net Income

If all small businesses were required to use a standard set of accounting practices – something like the rules applied by the Securities and Exchange Commission (SEC) for publicly traded corporations – it would be fairly easy to determine cash flow. And this could apply to the local fried chicken franchise, the carpet cleaning service, the soft drink bottling company, the shoe-shine stand on the corner and every other owner-operated enterprise. But that's not the case. (And considering that so many small business entrepreneurs are adamant about doing things their own way, it's unlikely that the imposition of a single system of accounting rules for them will ever be adopted).

Examples of the inconsistencies in reporting methods are plentiful. Many closely held corporations continue to show losses on the books even though the owners are able to live quite lavishly. And other businesses report profits, yet their owners can't find as much as a dime in the cash drawer.

As a business owner, you recognize that there are cash benefits to your operation which are not reflected on the profit and loss statement. If you add up items such as the company paid car and insurance (to the extent covering non-business travel), the funds set aside for depreciation that exceed actual replacement expenses, and the saleable inventory and equipment that have been written off the books but still exist, you will arrive at a sum that can be considered your "add backs." This figure, added to the profit shown for your business and any salary you take, represents the cash flow you would report when selling your business.

Since there are so many ways to conduct this calculation, you'll have a hard time finding a single formula that applies in all cases and exactly matches the circumstances of your business. Your accountant or a skilled business broker will be able to help you determine the figure you can call "adjusted net income" when your business is offered for sale.

At the end of this chapter is a P&L statement from a hypothetical business – the kind of statement that would be submitted with the corporate tax return. And there's a "recast" P&L noting which expense categories listed under the heading of operating costs, actually describe funds that don't get spent on the business, but go to the owner. These funds don't look like profits on the financial statement, and they aren't subject to the taxation that is imposed on profits, but they are used to benefit the owner just the same.

We need the total of all these funds if we're to establish a business value based on the most important criteria used in valuation – the amount of money the owner will receive from the business – that is, the adjusted net income.

Cash requirements can influence the value

The terms of a deal almost always impact what a buyer is willing to pay for a business. If you insist on an all-cash transaction when you sell your business, for example, you might expect to receive up to 25% less than the price you would get if you financed one-third to one-half the price. One explanation for this is that fewer buyers will have ready funds to meet your requirements and have working capital. So you'll need to shave the price to meet a smaller buyer pool.

Another explanation is that the multiple used in pricing a business is influenced by risk. Having to put up the entire purchase price of a business, carries with it an increased risk of loss, or at least the perception of an increase in the risk – maybe because the seller's insistence on all cash is an indication he or she thinks the buyer won't succeed.

Naturally, the size of the cash down payment required is only one factor with an impact on business valuation.

Price Adjustments: Terms of the Deal, Extra Assets, Unusual Circumstances, Quick Sale

The characteristics that can alter the starting point of value determination are varied and numerous. For our purposes however, there are a few common issues impacting the value of a business that deserve attention.

It was noted earlier that the terms of a deal can influence the final number. And we'll take up that matter in some detail in the next chapter.

And rather than cite only examples of over-priced listings, I might mention that there have been instances where a buyer was able to purchase a company at a below-market value having been in the right place at the right time. This can be an exception to the rule of "no great deals" expressed earlier. It occurs when a sale must be completed quickly because of death or illness of a principal. And the increased motivation of the seller for any number of reasons can result in a lower price than might have been accepted under normal circumstances.

If a capital infusion will be needed soon after the buyer takes over – to replace faltering equipment, for example – the business selling price might be depressed as a result. And the reverse is true. Sometimes an abundance of capital equipment can help a seller ask for and get a higher price than the usual multiple might dictate. The seller would argue that there's more assets to sell if needed, thereby reducing the business's downside risk. Besides, the additional machinery might enable the company to be even more productive and efficient and further prolong the useful life of the company's present infrastructure. A seller might also be able to boost the selling price a bit by promising to stay on without pay for awhile to help manage and to insure the buyer's success.

Is your business in a growth industry? Does your business confer on the owner any special opportunities or benefits that make it particularly desirable? These and other positive factors can result in a multiple of four or higher, being used to assess the value of what you have to sell.

Making your business less interesting, of course, is a short term lease for a location-sensitive enterprise, a declining market for your products or services, and other conditions that might increase the risk and/or reduce the appeal of your company.

Another set of factors has to do with the ease of management. If most anyone can stand behind the cash register and collect money, there will be a larger market of potential buyers and hence, a willingness to pay a higher price for your convenience store or retail shop. If special skills or particularly long hours are involved in running the business, however, its value probably will be negatively impacted.

And what about businesses that can be run absentee? If the seller truly does not need to be present for much of the day, the business might command a higher price than one that demands full time involvement on the part of the owner.

These are a few examples of factors that can influence the price of a business – probably just the tip of an iceberg-sized history of how buyer and seller accommodations and changes have affected values in transactions for small businesses in the U.S.

Additionally, it might be instructive for sellers to be aware of a couple of pricing strategies that are helpful if you want to get the full value for your company and aren't satisfied with the approaches suggested. Buyers also should be aware of these approaches as you may encounter them in your review of businesses for sale.

The EarnOut

Perhaps the best way to explain this way of defining the price of a business is by giving an example of the distribution company that was sold according to an earnout formula.

Because this well established firm was highly profitable, and required very little in the way of working capital, the owner asked a price that was nearly five times the annual income he collected.

The buyer was very impressed with the operation but a bit worried about the fact that there were virtually no hard assets to be included. If he were to fail, there would be nothing of value remaining from his investment.

The final deal called for half the price to be paid in cash, with the seller taking back the balance over a five-year period. It was agreed that the remaining amount owed on the business would be adjusted according to the buyer's subsequent gross profit. If the business was as lucrative over the payoff period as the seller promised, the seller would receive his full purchase price with interest. If there was a drop-off in gross profit, the seller's payments would be adjusted downward, accordingly. It was a workable solution for parties to the agreement because it addressed their issues. The broker however, was frustrated with this approach, as his commission was based on the purchase price and he had to wait 60 months to finish collecting his fee.

Letting the Market Determine Price

This strategy, perhaps inspired by techniques for selling real estate during hot markets, involves setting a deadline for offers, then inviting all interested buyers to submit the top price they're willing to pay by that date. This is similar to an auction with all interested participants encouraged to submit their maximum bid. The method works best in a situation where there are a number of prospective buyers who are motivated to own the company being offered. The benefit for the seller is that the maximum price might come out of this competitive process, without the need for a lot of negotiations and with a low risk of selling too low, too quickly. While this can be an effective tactic to achieve the desired ends, it should be handled by a broker experienced in this type of sale, so as to keep it orderly and to complete it successfully.

Valuing Unreported Income

Some sellers, while discussing the value of their business, get on the subject of having a buyer pay for income not recognized anywhere in the business' books. They want to know how that can be done.

And buyers want to know how to consider unreported income when evaluating a company's correct selling price.

My advice: Forget about it!

There are a number of reasons that a seller does not want to discuss unreported income with a purchaser, beginning with the fact that your prospective buyer may be an IRS agent engaged in the government's campaign to catch tax cheats. If you're still not convinced it's a bad idea to brag to a buyer about the money you siphon, consider the possibility of a disagreement with that person resulting in a lawsuit.

Will you settle up at less-than-favorable terms so the other party doesn't spill your secret? Or will you go to court and watch the judge, jury, attorneys and witnesses hear testimony about how you explained the technique you've developed for laundering cash in your business?

And even if there are no consequences on the order of a legal dispute, do you really want to have a good buyer learn about your dishonesty and then worry about your trustworthiness in the rest of the deal?

A seller can't have it both ways. If you're realizing net income without tax consequences it's not appropriate to claim it as part of your cash flow. If you want to sell your small business based on the total of your earnings, they should show up in your records.

And I advise buyers to have the same attitude expressed here. If the seller's records don't show evidence of the extra income that is claimed, then you're justified in assuming that it does not exist.

Conclusion

A discussion of this subject – determining the right price at which to sell or to buy a small business – could easily fill volumes of textbooks. For our purposes, the objective is to provide a brief overview.

A useful way for both the seller and the buyer to understand the probable market value for a business is to look at the problem from the point of view of someone who will work in the business as the owner/operator. In other words, this approach takes the side of the buyer who needs a certain level of return on his or her investment of time, labor and money.

That expectation is translated into a multiple that can vary according to a number of different factors affecting the business. The multiple is then computed with the anticipated adjusted net earnings to arrive at an initial figure to use in determining the price.

Other factors, including motivation of the parties, condition of the business, and deal structure, have an influence on the initial price, "fine tuning" it to a value that is likely to predict the final price at which a buyer and seller will agree.

And sellers who wonder how to include unreported cash for purposes of pricing their business are advised to forget it!

KEY POINTS FROM THIS CHAPTER

❖ Pricing a business correctly for sale continues to be a challenge with many economists and finance experts offering different theories about how to do it.

❖ It's a mistake to use principles involving the valuation of real property to try to determine what a small business is worth. That's because the comparables mechanism doesn't work with small businesses. For one thing, no two businesses are comparable.

❖ And it's not accurate to evaluate a small business along the same lines as one would a passive investment, such as the purchase of stock in a publicly held corporation.

❖ The best approach toward valuation of a small business is to look at the problem from the point of view of a typical buyer and determine what would be a reasonable return on the time and money the buyer invests in the business.

❖ Calculating a multiple of the earnings is a useful way to compute a business's value as it represents a balance of market supply and demand.

❖ Also a subject of differing opinions is the matter of measuring cash flow. A seller might benefit by discussing with an accountant or experienced business broker how to determine this figure for his or her business.

❖ Influencing values are a number of factors including risk, the terms of a deal (how much cash down is required), future of the industry, involvement of the seller, ease of management, amount of working capital that will be needed, and other issues that can impact success for the new owner.

❖ Review the next chapter for more ideas and information about how the terms of a transaction often can influence its price.

❖ The EarnOut strategy may help a buyer and seller arrive at a program for sale of the company that protects the buyer on the downside, and rewards the seller for the continuation of robust revenues.

❖ *Some sellers can avoid negotiations and perhaps, achieve the maximum price obtainable, when they ask that interested buyers make their best offer by a certain date. This is an auction process that should be handled only by experienced brokers.*

❖ *There's a simple answer for sellers wondering how to "price" the business' income that doesn't get reported: It is, "forget it!"*

Phiquex Manufacturing

Profit and Loss FY 2004

Category	Item	$ Amount	%
INCOME			
	From operations	626,812.00	
	Other (consulting)	11,000.00	
	Returns/Allowances	486.00	
	Gross Revenues	**$637,326.00**	**1.00**
EXPENSES			
	Cost of Goods:		
	Labor	190,405.60	0.299
	Materials	81,577.72	0.128
	Total	271,983.32	.427
	Gross Profit	**$365,342.68**	
	Overhead:		
	Advertising/promotion	8,922.56	0.014
	Administrative	7,647.91	0.012
	Auto	5,735.93	0.009
	Bank Charges	637.32	0.001
	Depreciation/Ammort	10,834.54	0.017
	Health coverage	13,383.84	0.021
	Insurance	19,757.10	0.031
	Interest	10,197.21	0.016
	Janitorial	25,493.04	0.04
	Legal/Accounting	12,109.19	0.019
	Maintenance	7,010.58	0.011
	Miscellaneous	7,647.91	0.012
	Office/Computer	14,021.17	0.022
	Officer Salary	18,000.00	0.028
	Payroll services	4,461.28	0.007
	Rent	52,898.06	0.083
	Selling Expenses	12,746.52	0.02
	Shipping/Handling	17,207.80	0.027
	Supplies	11,471.88	0.018
	Travel	3,823.96	0.006
	Utilities	29,954.32	0.047
	Total Expenses	**$293,962.12**	**0.461**
Net Income		**$ 71,380.56**	**0.112**

Phiquex Manufacturing

...acks to Compute Adjusted Net Income (Recast Financials)

Advertising/promotion	8,922.56	Sponsored Little League Team	1,200.00
Administrative	7,647.91	Sister's help running errands	3,250.00
Auto	5,735.93	Personal use est. 80%	4,589.00
Bank Charges	637.32		
Depreciation/Ammort	10,834.54	50% unneeded reserve	5,417.27
Health coverage	13,383.84	For officer and family	13,383.84
Insurance	19,757.10		
Interest	10,197.21		
Janitorial	25,493.04		
Legal/Accounting	12,109.19	Est. 25% for officer's personal	3,027.30
Maintenance	7,010.58		
Miscellaneous	7,647.91		
Office/Computer	14,021.17		
Officer Salary	18,000.00	Officer Salary	18,000.00
Payroll services	4,461.28		
Rent	52,898.06		
Selling Expenses	12,746.52	Personal Entertainment ($300/mo)	3,600.00
Shipping/Handling	17,207.80		
Supplies	11,471.88		
Travel	3,823.96	50% personal travel at trade show	1,912.00
Utilities	29,954.32		
Net Income	**$71,380.56**	**Total Add Backs**	**$54,379.41**
		Adjusted Net Income (Net Income + Total Add Backs)	**$125,759.97**

PLEASE NOTE THAT THIS INFORMATION REPRESENTS THE IDEAS OF THE SELLER AS TO WHAT CONSTITUTES ADJUSTED NET INCOME. BUYERS ARE URGED TO DISCUSS THIS ANALYSIS WITH THEIR ACCOUNTANTS AND TO DISCUSS WITH TAX ATTORNEYS THE TAX IMPLICATIONS REGARDING THE REPORTING OF INFORMATION.

THE SELLER DOES NOT REPRESENT THAT HE IS GIVING OUT, IN THE CONTEXT OF THIS INFORMATION, ANY ACCOUNTING OR TAX ADVICE.

CHAPTER SEVEN

WHAT'S THE RIGHT PRICE?
A FACTOR IS THE DEAL STRUCTURE

Having reviewed some approaches to pricing a small business in the previous chapter, and having touched on key pricing components, such as Adjusted Net Income, it's now appropriate to focus on pricing in a more macroeconomic sense. Specifically, it's important for buyers and sellers to understand pricing in terms of what you really are striving for in a sale – maximum economic benefit.

There can, in fact, be a difference for a seller between getting your price when the deal is signed, and still being satisfied – perhaps months or years later – that you received the best possible return from the sale of your business.

And if you, as a buyer, thought you came out ahead when you squeezed every excess dollar out of the asking price with your clever negotiating, you also ought to calculate the loss you incurred by not getting any post-sale cooperation from the seller – a seller offended by your negotiating tactics.

It is because of the importance of other issues involved and intertwined with the question of establishing price, that the entire picture needs to be brought to the attention of sellers and buyers involved in transactions by which small businesses change hands.

Establishing the Down payment

If a buyer has the opportunity to leverage into a business with a down payment and a promise to pay the balance to the seller over a period of time, there's more incentive to make the purchase. That will translate into a higher price than an all-cash requirement.

The down payment can influence price the way a cash requirement affects the desirability of anything that's for sale. As you crank up the down payment threshold, the number of qualified and interested buyers dwindles. And that translates immediately into softer demand which, in turn, tends to bring down the value of what's offered. The lesson of this economic principle for a business seller is that if you want to get your substantial price, you need to be flexible on the terms by which that price is paid.

Do you believe in the future of your business? If you insist on most of the cash at the close of escrow, it may be for any number of reasons. Regardless of your rationale, the buyer is likely to conclude that you want out, with minimum ties, because you see doom ahead. That's not a healthy message to send when someone's considering the purchase of your business.

Is it costly for a seller to insist on getting cashed out? As noted earlier, it's not uncommon for sellers who insist on an all-cash deal to receive roughly three-fourths of the sum that they might have gotten in a deal that offered a substantial amount of financing. That's a 25% discount, like buying a $200,000 business for $150,000.

And buyers as well as seller should be aware that even if a deal looks like it requires all, or most of the cash at the beginning, there frequently are alternatives which might serve to provide a more manageable package for the buyer and result in a higher price for the seller.

The owner of a bookstore, for example, was ready to retire and wanted a sizable down payment, explaining that she needed to satisfy the debt on the company's computer system and inventory management software, and to eliminate a payables balance to vendors. "I want to make sure everything is free and clear for a new buyer," she told the broker.

The answer to this problem was, of course, quite simple. The obligations represented a neat little financing vehicle. The deal was structured to include, in the price, the assumption of the seller's debt. With a more reasonable offering package, she was able to find a buyer who was pleased with the low down payment requirement. He used his cash to invest in a promotion campaign which improved the store's sales. And the business' cash flow enabled him to quickly pay off the seller's obligations that the buyer had assumed.

Other sellers have maintained they needed the purchase price all at once because the money was earmarked for an investment – in one case the down payment on a retirement home. Another seller had his eye on an expensive European sports car. Once the reasons for the cash down payment requirements were voiced, we were able to develop a strategy that met their needs, including getting their businesses sold. Each seller raised the needed money from a bank and serviced the new debt using payments coming from the buyer under their freshly-minted seller financing programs.

Sellers may complain that this adds a bit of work and may cost a few dollars in the interest spread (between what is paid to the lender and collected from the buyer) but most see these costs as well worth the benefit of a completed deal at the desired price.

And I've heard sellers object, bluntly, to financing a deal because of the fear the buyer won't succeed in the business and will fail to make payments. That's not a happy prospect. It makes me wonder if it's time to restructure the offering to reflect the seller's bleak outlook. Or maybe a more competent buyer will solve the problem.

I think it's clear that in the push and pull of negotiations over the price and payoff scheme for a small business, some flexibility on the part of either party can win them concessions in the price. More lenient terms offered by the seller often come packaged with the request that the purchaser meet the asking price. And if you're a buyer intent on getting a lower price than asked, you might be able to get agreement on the reduction by emphasizing your willingness to put more than is asked into a down payment, or by agreeing to discharge the balance with substantial payments that clear it more quickly than the seller had anticipated

Incidentally, sellers whose businesses require a lot of working capital will be more likely to get their price by offering the buyer easy terms. For example, if the new owner will have to finance receivables and carry a large inventory, the seller will be more likely to get his asking price if it can be handled with a down payment that is one-half or less, and manageable terms for the balance. A seller who forgets about the cash needs of an incoming owner, and who forgets that the new owner will want to measure the return against the entire cash outlay (not just the down payment) is likely to set a price that's out of reach of the market.

I'm a strong advocate for seller financing being part of a transaction whenever possible – particularly considering that the majority of sellers who think they need most of their cash at the start, actually have alternatives. The biggest need for cash when an enterprise changes hands is usually with the business itself, so the buyer can deal with unexpected expenses and invest in promotions to generate more business. When sellers think through this issue, they generally agree that the continuation of the business in a healthy state is in their best interests as well as the best interests of their buyers.

How Payments to a Seller Can be Structured

Not only down payment, but other aspects of a deal structure can impact the price. In the midst of a marketing campaign involving a dry cleaning business a few years ago, a layer of uncertainty was added to the mix when the seller's landlord announced plans for a major remodel of the shopping center. Had this action been imminent, the seller might have elected to wait out the construction and disruption of business, and then re-energize his selling efforts once the facility was back in full operation. But the project wasn't scheduled to begin for 18 months, and might be delayed beyond that. The seller, suffering health problems and eager to retire, was uncertain what to tell prospective buyers. They wanted to know, of course, not only when the construction would begin, but also how long it would go on and what impact it would have on business. And although the landlord had promised to offer tenants some rent relief to lessen the impact of lost revenue, it was not clear how helpful that would be.

When an interested and motivated buyer was found, a deal was worked out with seller financing for half the purchase price over a four year period. It was agreed that during the construction, the buyer's monthly payments to the seller would be reduced by a ratio equal to the percentage drop-off in business recorded the prior month. For example, if the August sales were 25% less than the prior, pre-construction August, the buyer's September payment would be 75% of the standard monthly amount. In this case, the final selling price would not be determined until the end of the four-year obligation. By allowing payments – and ultimately, the price – to "float" with business revenues, the seller was able to conclude a transaction in a timely manner, even in the face of these future unknowns.

In some circumstances where a new owner would be strapped for cash for the first few months after taking over, there has been cooperation by sellers agreeing to wait three months, even six months before the buyer was required to begin making payments on the obligation created by seller financing. Another approach has been designed for a situation where a business risks failure at some future time. Perhaps a big-box competitor is rumored to be moving into the area. Maybe the landlord has not yet committed to a lease renewal past the expiration coming in a few years. The reasoning in these cases is that if the worst happens, the seller would have been out of business anyway. So provisions can be included in the sales contract allowing the buyer to call for cancellation of the seller-financed note, and stop making payments, if the business must be discontinued or cut back dramatically.

This creative approach – really a variation of the earnout strategy – usually includes a low price because of the risk that the buyer won't have a business to sell, and eventually will lose the investment. But, of course, the price isn't definitive until the end of the obligation to the seller, because price is related to the payments, and they are adjusted on the basis of what happens in the future.

In these situations the right price is a changeable number, meant to reflect real circumstances over time. Although it isn't the solution in every case in which there are questions about what will happen in the future – and not everyone is flexible enough to see the benefits of this approach – it is a very effective way to please the buyer and seller who want their agreed-on price to be correct when reflecting on it in the future as well as in the present..

The interaction of price and seller terms in a transaction for a small business can impact the way a note is structured.

Suppose a seller reluctantly agrees to carry back part of a purchase price on a profitable business so the buyer can use her limited cash to fuel the company's continued growth. The payoff might be set up with large payments over a short period of time – that is, the debt is retired quickly. The benefit for the buyer is avoiding a cash-strapping down payment so there's money to make sure the business stays on a success track. And the seller wins with a satisfactory transaction, the payoff handled rather rapidly, plus the likelihood that the business – which secures the debt, and is cash-strong to begin with – will remain healthy.

In many of these cases, as the terms are adjusted, the price is affected as well. It's not unusual for a fast payoff schedule – as in the example just cited – to be linked with a lowered price. And the reverse can be true. If the seller agrees to let the buyer take plenty of time retiring the financing, the incentive might be expressed in a full-price deal. In effect, the seller is saying: "Okay, you can stretch out my payments and make your monthly obligation pretty low, but you have to meet my price."

What is the Best Collateral for the Seller Who Carries Back Part of the Purchase Price

Another piece of the puzzle forming the picture of a complete transaction has to do with the choice of collateral. In other words, what will secure the debt to a seller who finances part of the purchase price? In most cases a note to the seller is collateralized by the assets of the business. And that's usually fine with the buyer. "After all," the purchaser reasons, "if the seller believes the business is good, he should have no problem about accepting it as security for the loan."

Not every seller sees it this way, however. Consider someone who's built a successful, profitable small business and now wants to retire, expecting the proceeds from the business sale to provide the funds needed for the seller's later years. The outgoing owner has agreed to carry back part of the purchase price to make the business more desirable and to yield a good selling price. The problem comes in when it's the business itself that is suggested as security for what will be the major portion of the seller's income.

The seller in this case has a concern – a legitimate one – that the retirement planning, everything worked for over years of building the business, is riding on the success of the new owner. Suppose the owner fails, through no fault of the business. There can be a health problem, a natural disaster and any number of circumstances that impact the buyer and that would have the effect of ruining the seller's financial future. "How about a piece of property for security? Maybe your home?" suggests the seller.

As you might conclude, both parties' worries should be addressed in order to have a transaction that works for everyone. What to do? The place for compromise might be in the sales price. And indeed, the solution sometimes is an adjustment in price to reflect the risk/reward dynamic involved in this dilemma. If granted the concession of a lower price for the business, the buyer might be willing to put up a piece of real estate, such as a second mortgage on the family home, to satisfy the seller's feelings of insecurity. Alternatively, a boosted price might make the seller breath easier about this issue, and be willing to assume the risk, because of the enhanced reward.

Another way to deal with this problem is to have part, but not all of the obligation to the seller backed up with collateral other than the business. The buyer can agree to make payments on two notes (for the amount carried back), one of which is collateralized by the subject business, the other backed up by a trust deed in real property or the pledge of other assets.

Tax Impact of a Business Sale Affects Pricing

Stephen, owner of a manufacturing company, had a round figure in mind that he wanted to net from the sale of his business. Most of the people willing to meet his price felt that much of the value of the enterprise resided in his contacts in the industry. Their offers allocated much of the price to his agreement to introduce the new owner to customers, and his promise to refrain from engaging in that business as a competitor for five years following close. The problem, as Stephen learned from his tax accountant, is that the IRS would consider the money allocated this way to be a salary, and it would be subject to taxation as ordinary income – at a high rate.

He'd hoped to have a buyer agree to the idea that purchase of his equipment would represent most of the price. He could then deduct the equipment's book value from the allocated amount, and the difference would be subject to taxation at the lower, capital gains rate. That way he'd net what he wanted.

Because Stephen's method of allocation was not beneficial to the interested buyers, they declined to meet his requirement.

Stephen finally worked out a deal designed to provide him the most after-tax benefit from the sale. The allocation was skewed toward Stephen's preferred tax structure, but he had to lower his price. He didn't meet his goal but came as close as possible given the tax situation. And the key was the downward adjustment in the total value of the assets – in other words a lower price.

Flexibility Helps Achieve Agreements

A nice round number to brag about. Security for the golden years. The knowledge that the business will continue to be healthy. A good income for the next few years. Keeping the largest share of the sale proceeds allowable under tax law.

These and other considerations enter into the planning you must do when placing your company on the market for sale, and when determining the value – that is, the price to ask for the business.

As the reader has likely determined, the sales price for a business is not set in a vacuum. It is a function of this overall package of benefits for the buyer and seller.

The most successful sellers keep in mind their ultimate objective: Selling the business and receiving the maximum economic benefit warranted by all of the circumstances involved at the time. There's no value in almost selling the business at a terrific price. Nor does a seller want to get a deal that doesn't yield at least most of the economic benefit anticipated.

And the buyer, who will profit by taking over a company he or she has selected after a long search and careful evaluation, is wise to negotiate for the purchase with the idea of achieving a win-win result. You usually can look forward to valuable post-sale support if the seller is treated with respect throughout the process.

Whether you're a buyer or seller, you probably understand the point that a participant in a business deal who is flexible about the interplay of the factors – including, but not limited to price – involved in a transaction, is often able to enjoy the maximum benefit from the sale.

Conclusion

Over the past two chapters we've reviewed the issue of price as it applies to the sale of a small business. First we analyzed the methods of assigning value and the components that are used in the computations when pricing a company. In this chapter the reader is offered examples to illustrate the way price is merely one component in an overall business transaction. It's one piece of the puzzle. As the real goal of most sellers and buyers is to enjoy the maximum possible economic benefit in the transaction for a business, you are encouraged to understand the interaction of the payment terms, the tax treatment, and the deal structure that can work with price to help you achieve your objective.

KEY POINTS FROM THIS CHAPTER

❖ *It is important that sellers understand the pricing of a small business in terms of what you really are striving for in a sale. That is maximum economic benefit.*

❖ *Down payment relates to price of a business the way that the amount of cash required to buy anything affects the marketability of what's being sold. The more cash needed, the fewer likely buyers. And that can mean a lower value.*

❖ *An all-cash requirement on the part of the seller can mean that he or she will have to offer a discount of up to 25% off the asking price to achieve an agreement. This is because only some buyers will agree to put all cash into a deal.*

❖ *One reason that buyers are reluctant to pay the price all in cash to a seller is that if the buyer runs into a problem with the business and could use some assistance from the seller, that aid is not likely to be provided; the seller is completely out of the deal and has no motivation to cooperate.*

❖ *Willingness of the seller to help you by financing part of the purchase price raises the perceived value of that business – if only because the seller's message is that he or she trusts you will do well enough, at least, to meet your obligations.*

❖ *An attractive deal structure involves a down payment of 30% to 50%, and a three to seven-year period to make payments to the seller at a market rate of interest in monthly installments.*

❖ *My experience is that most sellers who think they need all or most of the price of a business as down payment can find other ways to meet their cash needs. It usually is to their benefit to take less down and provide financing.*

❖ *I advocate seller financing wherever possible as I've learned it usually leads to successful deals where the business continues in a healthy condition and all parties win.*

❖ *Not only down payment, but other aspects of a deal structure can impact price. A transaction for a dry cleaning company example was offered to illustrate how the price was dependent on future events, and could be changed through the mechanism of adjustable payments that were influenced by these events.*

❖ *Other alternatives in deal structure include a fast payoff, which can be balanced with a lower price; or a longer payoff tied to a higher price.*

❖ *The choice of collateral provided to a seller who carries back some purchase price is another part of a transaction that works together with price. A buyer usually feels the business should represent the security; the seller may want other assets. The resolution of this dilemma can sometimes be found in an adjustment of the price to accommodate the parties.*

❖ *If there is a difference of opinion between a buyer and seller as to what collateral should be used to secure the buyer's obligation, one solution is to include two notes, one secured by the business and the other secured by the buyer's real estate.*

❖ *Additionally, tax considerations can result in adjustment of price. One party gaining favorable tax treatment may need to give on the price issue and visa versa. Sellers are advised to remember the final selling price does not define their ultimate benefit. Maximum return on the sale, after taxes, is usually what you're after.*

❖ *The most successful sellers keep their desired objectives in mind and remember there's no value in almost selling the business at a terrific price, or in successfully getting a deal, but not in a way that gets you at least close to the maximum economic benefit.*

CHAPTER EIGHT

SELLER'S GUIDE: OFFERING YOUR BUSINESS FOR SALE

If you're interested in selling your small business, and you have followed some of the advice and ideas offered – organized your papers, discussed and planned the offering with your attorney and accountant, perhaps selected a broker (if you want professional representation), talked things over with your landlord and other people whose cooperation you'll need, then decided on an asking price, and set out the terms – you have managed most of the things over which you have substantial control. Now, embarking on the marketing campaign will expose you to the uncertainty in this process. From now on you probably will have less influence than you'd like, not only over the reaction of the market to your business for sale, but also the willingness of prospects to make an offer and of buyers to accept your terms.

So you'll do well to manage, as much as you can, the events and outcome of the marketing efforts. Here are some ideas to guide you in the conduct of your campaign. And you'll likely find this information useful to know even if you are turning the responsibility over to a business broker.

Controlled Exposure

The key to getting the best offer on most anything being sold is, of course, to expose it to the largest possible audience of buyers. In any given population of prospects, a certain percentage will have an interest in your offering. The more prospects who are informed about it, the more possible customers with whom you can work.

One distinguishing characteristic about promoting a small business for sale however, is the need to practice a high degree of discrimination in the choice of your prospects. Most likely you don't want it generally known that the company is being marketed. It's nearly always a bad business practice to let customers, employees, vendors and competitors discover that the business is for sale, and for them to learn about details of your operation.

The challenge then is to broadcast the availability of your business as widely as possible, still keeping it a secret from those individuals who somehow have a connection with the business. You don't want everyone to know your business is for sale – only those people who have no dealings with your enterprise, and who have the financial capability and other qualifications needed to own it.

This is indeed an interesting marketing problem. And there is no sure fire solution.

But there is a strategy commonly practiced by most sellers and business brokers and agents that has proved, over time, to represent the most effective approach. The idea is to consider your promotion program to be a process conducted in phases. The first phase is launched with a broad, general announcement of the company being for sale, and only the most basic information provided. The final phase is a face-to-face-conference in which a qualified prospective buyer – whom you have ascertained is not an employee, regular customer or known competitor – receives proprietary information about your offering in return for a written promise to treat this information confidentiality, not disclosing it to anyone other than the prospective buyer's advisors. And there are interim phases in which you qualify the prospect, while the prospect is learning more about what you offer and deciding whether to pursue it.

I call this process the "dance." It's based on an exchange of information, the give and take of two parties discovering, little-by-little, if there is a mutual interest in doing business. It ends when one of the two parties, or perhaps both, determines there isn't sufficient interest in pursuing the exchange. At that point the interaction will terminate. The other possible outcome of the dance is that your prospect wants to purchase the business, has the ability to do so, and meets your price and terms, or works out with you a mutually agreeable deal.

The Critical First 30-60 Days

Small business owners who want to sell should be aware that the way your company is presented during the first month or two is vital to the success of your sales campaign. Like every other business broker and consultant who's been working in the industry for any length of time, I've seen numerous situations in which a perfectly salable business has not been matched up with a suitable buyer after months of marketing. Usually it's because the seller or the seller's representative "dropped the ball" early in the effort. Seeing the same ad in the paper, week after week, is a clue that the business has been improperly marketed from the beginning. Another clue is to hear from a qualified, serious buyer that a broker or seller neglected to respond to an inquiry about a business being offered. Still another is to learn about buyers becoming impatient as they wait to make an offer on a business as soon as they receive the added information promised, but not delivered, by the seller or seller's representative.

Don't lose good buyers by your lack of preparation or inattentiveness to their requests. The longer your business sits on the market, even if the reason is because of your inattention, the more dubious the offering will appear.

Have you ever declined to purchase something you liked because it seemed "shop worn?" Did you ask: "If this is such a good deal, why hasn't someone else bought it already?" If you've had that experience, you understand how a prospective buyer might be uninterested in purchasing your business simply because it has been available for what seems a long time.

Put off the beginning of your marketing program if you have to wait for more records or a confirmation about a lease request. But don't launch your business sales effort as you would a rocket, then let it sputter out before it has a chance to reach orbit, while you try to figure out how to respond to inquiries.

Let's review the basic process of exposing your business, and touch on some of the components that make up your campaign.

Advertising

While some brokers feel that general circulation newspapers represent one of the best vehicles for advertising your business for sale, other say they have unsatisfactory results this way, preferring to rely on online business promotion services, such as *www.USABizMart.com* Others who specialize in particular kinds of businesses try to focus their marketing campaigns with ads in trade periodicals and with contacts at trade associations. The best strategy, if you have the time, patience and resources, is to reach as many outlets as possible where you feel you might be able to interest prospective buyers – qualified ones – in your business.

I advocate that sellers commit to a budget of $2,000 to $3,000 for advertising in print and web-based media. It may seem like a big investment, but if you want to receive your price and terms, assuming they are reasonably set for what you have to offer, you may need exposure to hundreds of possible prospects. I don't think it makes sense to try to save a little money when you want to get as many people as possible to investigate your offering. You want to generate a large response so that when the population is narrowed down, through the introduction and qualification process, there are some who remain interested and able to be your buyer.

Incidentally, one of the requirements you might have for your broker, if you are represented by one, is that he or she spends a certain sum on advertising over the life of the listing. In fact, there's no reason not to get this in writing as part of the listing contract. It's not unusual for a brokerage to earmark a few thousand dollars to promote a listing which is well prepared for a sale and will generate thousands of dollars in commissions if a deal is completed.

The local daily newspapers in most every part of the country carry business opportunities listings in their classified ad sections every day. Pick the one that best covers your area, and use it to promote your selling solicitation.

And whether your ad is distributed in printed or electronic classified sections, or both, make sure it includes the best features of your offering so as to increase the chances of getting good responses. Here are some of the phrases likely to provoke an interest on the part of a buyer and get your phone to ring:

Absentee owner

Continued history of earnings growth

Long established

Good business records

Great lease

Flexible landlord

Very profitable

Priced to sell

Good seller financing

Low down payment

Seller training included

Franchise opportunity

EZ Terms

Fortune 500 customers

Super location

Excellent, new equipment

Real estate included

This list of catch phrases is as potent on the Internet as in print. Your ads with a web-based service will probably include more information than the 3 or 4-line newspaper ad. And your Internet advertising can usually include a photo, or the corporate logo, if you're selling a known franchise. The added graphic is helpful in getting attention of prospective buyers. That can be important, because getting a reader's attention can be a difficult thing to do considering that in many media there are so many displays competing for a reader's attention.

Broker Network

I recently spoke with a seller who felt that it would not be right to let business brokers know about his business for sale, because he had not listed it with a broker. I don't agree. There's no reason you can't contact brokerages with buyers seeking businesses to let them know what you offer. Some brokers and agents represent buyers only, and are paid by the buyer upon successful completion of a transaction. The more businesses these professionals are aware of, the better. And there's no reason you can't negotiate with a broker to bring you the eventual buyer for a few percentage points more than you're asking and keep the difference as a fee. You may even be agreeable to the idea of designating half of a full commission from your proceeds to pay a broker who brings the buyer willing and able to meet your terms.

As you can see, there are a number of ways to approach the idea of getting a broker's help in finding a buyer, even if you are representing yourself and saving the listing brokerage fee. An active business broker has something you don't have – a current database of qualified buyers. By working with a broker, or brokers who would represent the buyer, you can access that resource without having to give up a full brokerage fee.

Meanwhile, don't neglect to connect with chambers of commerce, business networking organizations and other business-related social opportunities to meet prospective buyers or, perhaps someone with a brother-in-law or friend who would be the perfect new owner for your business. I've known sellers to flush out good buyers by doing their networking at alumni groups and even by posting a notice at union halls and vocational schools that teach a curriculum related to the subject of your business. And if your business is a franchise, don't forget to check with your franchisor for leads of people who have inquired about an opportunity in your area.

Initial Qualifying

An early step is for you to establish a way for people to contact you. A dedicated telephone number obtained simply for this purpose will allow you to get calls from interested parties, and they won't know (until you're ready to tell them) whom they're contacting. This is clearly preferable to giving your business phone number (there goes your secret!) or your home number (where your caller will hear the barking dog and blasting video games and then leave a return number with one of the forgetful teens in your house). An answering machine or voice mail message should be attached to the number so if you can't answer, the caller gets a professional reception and is reassured that you'll respond promptly to the request. And then make sure you do so.

If you have a cell phone usually with you, it doesn't hurt to place that number in the ad as well. You can't make it too easy for interested buyers to get in touch with you. You can always reject someone later if they are not serious or are otherwise unqualified. But initially you want to hear from as many people as possible.

Some sellers think it's sufficient to do business out of a post office box, rather than a phone number, as it gives prospects a way to communicate with you without knowing who you are. They appreciate this as quicker to get than a new phone number and less costly. I think this is a mistake. You need to communicate in a way that's easy for people to contact and respond to you. Another possibility is to set up an email account just for this purpose. Some people prefer to communicate this way, so you should have the capability of being reached and of responding to them on the Internet. My preference, however, is the telephone. I believe your communication, if it will lead to a sale, must be immediate and direct.

In your records it's a good idea to keep track of which ads are producing the most and the best calls. You may want to alter the campaign at some point, and the information about what outlets are producing the most qualified responses will help you to de-emphasize unproductive media so you can beef-up in the online media or the printed periodicals that are working best for you.

When first talking to a prospective buyer, whether you answered their call or phoned back after getting a message, you want to learn as much as you can – not only how to contact him or her, but also find out what the person is looking for.

If you're not in the habit of setting up a file for a project such as selling your business, make a note to yourself that you've just learned a useful idea. One of the folders in the file should contain a list of all the people you talk to, all of the information you've obtained about them and a note about what was discussed and when.

Before spending much time with this person, you want to try and determine if he or she is qualified as to financial ability and the skills to run your business. You also want to determine, right away, if the two of you are able to communicate productively in a way that might lead to a transaction for your business.

If the prospect is completely unwilling to tell you anything about them or their interests, this actually is effective communication. They are letting you know they won't participate in the "dance" (of information exchange). But it's not communication likely to help you sell the business, so you're probably well advised to cut that conversation short and go on to the next prospect.

We'll cover, in more detail, the questions to ask – and even offer some suggested scripts – when we take up the subject of qualifying prospects in a later chapter.

A response to your ad or an inquiry from a broker or business advisor in touch with possible buyers can all be handled the same way. Many sellers find it useful to send out, or fax (but not from your office) or email a one-page "blind profile" that gives the basic details about your business, without revealing the name, address or enough specifics to identify it (see the blind profile sample at the end of this chapter). Respond to the inquiry with that information, after getting the name and contact details for the person who asked. And encourage the party to contact you if they want to learn more.

Incidentally, I know of sellers who included, with the blind profile, a couple of blank forms – the non-disclosure agreement and a financial statement sheet. They explained that before getting into too much more detail about the business, they would require the non-disclosure commitment and would want to know more about the buyer's ability. I think this is an excellent way to begin the task of qualifying buyers – the subject covered in pages that soon follow.

I also advocate that your notes on each prospect with whom you've spoken be organized and easy to find in your file. And support these buyer records with a follow-up system keyed to your calendar so you're reminded to contact the person three or four days later. Ask if the prospect has any questions and if they are interested in pursuing it further.

Remember that you're engaged in the dance, and that you're prepared to provide more information in return for some answers to your questions about what they are looking for, what is their work experience and what is their price range.

Your prospect may have specific questions related to the facts provided on the blind profile and may want to know about information not covered, such as details of the financial performance, the number of hours you devote and your duties, the future of your industry and any problems you foresee in the business.

There also may be questions about how flexible you are in the price and terms, which may be a sign that the prospect lacks the financial ability to complete the deal. Or it may be an indication that you've got a prospect who wants to start negotiating before it has been established that he or she has a solid interest in buying the business.

A response I recommend for questions posed initially about your "flexibility" is to let the prospect know you would like to see a complete offer, and know about the financial ability and work experience of the person making the offer before commenting. You also can suggest that the person focus on one issue at a time. One comment I like is:" Don't you think it makes sense for you to learn more about the business, and if you're interested in it, before we get into negotiating? My accountant thinks this is quite fairly priced. If you decide you want to own this business, you'd be hurting your chances of beating out other buyers, by trying to get a lower price or better terms before you've had a chance to find out what it is really worth to you."

Another way of responding to the question about your willingness to "deal" is with your own question about the buyer's ability. "Is the down payment more than you can handle?"

Some of the other questions you might encounter as you begin to qualify prospective buyers, and some strategies for participating in this dance will be covered in greater detail in a later chapter.

The Package

Our focus here is on that phase of the process when you provide more information, selectively, and recommend a meeting (suggest a coffee shop or other public place) so you and the prospect can learn more about the possibility of doing business with one another.

As the blind profile was the primary tool used to respond to initial inquiries and engage the interest of prospects, the package is the collection of information about your business which you will use to further the dialog with the prospect and take the relationship to the next step. Included in the package is a more extensive profile, identifying the company and giving a brief review of its financials. (See the business profile at the end of this chapter.) Copies of financial information (P&L and balance sheet for the current year to date and the past three years), your asset list (with an appraisal of equipment if possible), your lease and other agreements you need to conduct business belong in the package as well. Another item to include is any newspaper or magazine articles you can find which support your assertion that your company is in a growth industry or in a healthy and growing geographic area. And franchise business owners will want to include some of the promotional material produced by your franchisor.

A description of the ideal buyer is an excellent addition to your package. What education, background and experience should someone have in order to be successful in the business? How much working capital? This inclusion is likely to provoke further interest in your offering on the part of buyers who have the requisite credentials. And it can provide an automatic screening function, making it less likely that you'll hear from – and have your time wasted by – people who are not qualified.

You may find that even before you send out, or hand out your package, that it is useful as a reference for responding to the questions posed by the prospective purchasers when you follow up after the initial contact. Tell the prospect you've got on the phone that you are reading from your documents, so you can explain things in more detail.

Then, your offer to present the entire package to the party, in person, brings you to the suggestion that you and the prospective buyer meet to exchange information.

And remember that it's never too soon to impress on prospects the importance of maintaining confidentiality about the offering. Some sellers think it's sufficient to mention it once, and get a signed non-disclosure agreement, then neglect to bring it up again, assuming the prospect got the message. I think you need to introduce early the idea that a buyer's respect for your confidentiality request is critically important to you. By repeating this theme and reminding buyers about it, you will lessen the chances of a leak during the marketing of your business.

Being the Bearer of Bad News

You'll notice, elsewhere in these pages, that I advocate being the source of any negative information that might be encountered by prospects who are learning about your business. An interested buyer probably will discover, during due diligence examination, any factors that are likely to impact the future of your company's sales or profits. Don't wait for that. Let prospects find out from you. By doing this, you'll earn the trust of buyers and you'll have a chance to explain negative information and put it in proper perspective. One seller whose retail business was at risk because of the "big box" competitor moving into the area, made sure to inform prospective buyers about this. Then he said he would help to craft an ad campaign for the buyer, emphasizing his company's service tradition and its other strengths, pointing out to customers the disadvantages of doing business with a large, nation-wide chain store, that had no real connection to the community.

Timing the release of less-than-positive information takes some careful thought. You don't want to discourage a prospective purchaser before he or she has a chance to become interested in your business. Many people, once they're enthused about something, will tolerate a certain amount of negative information. The same buyers learning this same information at the outset might have rejected the offering, because they hadn't yet developed an interest in it. On the other hand, you don't want to waste a lot of time with a motivated buyer who will pull out of the deal at the last minute, scared away when the bad news is finally revealed.

I advocate preparing a written disclosure stating the facts, and including your opinion about how the negative might be turned into a positive. The statement should be shown to the buyer as soon as you detect the person has a strong interest in the business.

Conclusion

The objective in this chapter has been to help the do-it-yourself business seller to get the word out about the offering, in a controlled manner, and then be in position to respond to questions and move the conversation along toward the next step. In a following chapter, we'll cover the process by which the prospective buyer learns more about the business and agrees to keep your secrets as well as revealing his or her financial ability, work history and general ability to be your buyer.

Throughout this process it is strongly recommended that you maintain an organized file of buyers containing complete notes about your contact with each. And hang onto those folders. I know of more than one occasion when a seller learned a deal in process would not go through, and went back to buyer information so as to contact other interested prospects and find someone else to purchase the business.

KEY POINTS FROM THIS CHAPTER

❖ *By following some of the suggestions offered in previous pages, you've had control over the early stages of the sales process. The uncertainty begins when you offer the business to the marketplace and wait to find out it there will be interest and positive reaction. Much of the chapter contains information to help you exert as much influence as possible on the process that follows.*

❖ *The interesting marketing problem you face is how to broadcast the availability of your business as widely as possible, still keeping it a secret from anyone whom you don't want to have the information. That includes employees, customers, vendors and competitors.*

❖ *The strategy for dealing with the marketing challenge is to conduct the process of marketing in phases, starting with initial introduction using a "blind profile" (the company is not identified). A later phase is to meet a prospective buyer and engage in the "dance" whereby each reveals a little information, then progressively more information, until it's determined either that you want to conduct negotiations with a transaction in mind, or that one or both of you don't want to do business.*

❖ *It can't be stressed enough how important the first 30 to 60 days of your campaign can be. If the initial offering of your business is mishandled, it can substantially increase the difficulty of finding the right buyer and ruin the likelihood of your getting a satisfactory deal in a short period of time. Don't lose good buyers because of lack of preparation or inattentiveness to their requests.*

❖ *A good advertising strategy, if you have the resources, is to run your business for sale ad in print as well as online media which cater to business buyers, such as www.USABizMart.com Don't skimp on advertising. It would be a shame not to get the best offer simply because there weren't enough qualified people aware of the availability of the business.*

❖ *Wherever your ads appear – print or electronic, or both – use words and phrases that are known to provoke interest. Emphasizing growing business, excellent income, good terms, good lease, well established and some of the other virtues listed in the chapter will help to make that phone ring in response to your ads.*

❖ *With their database of qualified buyers, brokers are an important resource even if you don't have the business listed. Get your blind profile to brokers so they can introduce the business to their clients. Some brokers represent buyers only and are paid to look for businesses like yours. Others might want to arrange with you to pay a half of the commission if they produce the buyer for your business. And it might be worth it to get a good buyer at your price and terms.*

❖ *You can't make it too easy for interested buyers to get in touch with you. Get a dedicated phone line so interested buyers seeing your ads can contact you. Make sure your line is equipped to take messages if you aren't available. Follow up immediately.*

❖ *Keep track of which advertising is working best, and is not working, in the event you want to modify your advertising campaign.*

❖ *Sellers are advised to start a file for sale of the business and to include information about all the inquiries. You never know when having this information will come in handy. For example, if you settle on a buyer who, it turns out, cannot perform on the agreement, won't you be glad you still have the contact information for the number two candidate?*

❖ *Follow up with those who've made an inquiry about your business and attempt to qualify them as to interest, financial strength and general ability to own your business.*

❖ *A more extensive profile of the business is for use when you meet with prospects and obtain their non-disclosure agreement. This business profile gives identifying information regarding your company, an overview of financial performance and – with the inclusion of relevant documents – details about your hard assets and your agreements with landlord, employees, customers and others.*

❖ *A description of the ideal buyer is a good component for inclusion in the package of information about your business. It can be a "turn-on" for those who have what it takes. And it will help to discourage unqualified people with whom you probably should not be spending time.*

❖ *Your disclosure of any negative factors that may affect your business, along with an explanation of how to deal with these problems, is a much better way to handle this kind of information than ignoring it and hoping buyers won't discover it. They will find out about it on their own, in most cases, and because you neglected to "manage" this news, you'll have little opportunity to put it into a context that can help soften the blow and keep the buyer on track.*

❖ *Samples of a blind profile and a business profile can be found at the end of the chapter to give you some ideas about information for inclusion in these documents.*

SAMPLE "BLIND" BUSINESS PROFILE

Manufacturer of Mechanical Devices used in Consumer Electronics

Long Established   Very Profitable   Business Growing

Established: **17 Years**   Location: **Santa Clara County (No. CA)**

Owner Responsibility: **Mgmt/Sales**   Reason for Sale: **Moving from area**

Number Employees: **Owner + 5 FT + 2 PT**   Lease Length: **6 yr + (2) 4 yr options**

Ownership: **"S" Corp**   Hours Operation: **M - Thu: 6:30 am - 4:00 pm, Fri: 6:30 am - 12 noon**

Performance: **$125,660 adjusted net profit on sales of $637,326 in most recently completed fiscal year**

Opportunity for buyer to cash in on growth of this industry with well-established company respected for the quality of its products sold to long-term "blue-chip" customers. Seller will train and introduce to clients and remain with Buyer to assist in smooth transition.

Asking Price: $ 350,000 (plus about $20,000 for inventory of parts and finished goods)

Terms: $ 140,000 cash down payment required
                         100,000 independent financing available for qualified buyers
                         110,000 seller carry back for 5 years
                                    at 4.5% interest; mo. payment of $2,050.73
                         _____
                         $ 350,000

Asset sale
Price includes: Machinery and Equipment: $143,000 at current book value
                         Leasehold improvements: 30,000 at current book value
                         Goodwill   140,000
                         Covenant not to Compete   37,000 for five years
                                                             _____
                         Total $350,000

Other: To be delivered to Buyer free and clear of obligations and payables. Working capital requirement: $100,000 estimated for: purchase inventory of parts and finished goods ($20,000), various tax and other deposits required from new owner ($5,000), accounts receivable funding ($65,000), working capital ($10,000).

                         For additional Information: Call seller, Lou, at 650 555.1234

SAMPLE: MORE COMPLETE BUSINESS PROFILE

Offered for sale

Phlquex Manufacturing
6789 Standard Business Street
San Jose, CA

For added Information:

Owner, Lou: 650 555.1234

Overview:

Opportunity to benefit from growth of this industry with well-established company known for the quality of its products sold to long-term "blue chip" customers. Seller will train and introduce buyer to clients and remain with business for a few weeks to assist in smooth transition.

Business information:

Established: 1988
Owner Responsibility: Manage operations, conduct sales
Reason for Sale: Seller moving from area
Number of Employees: Owner + 5 full-time + 2 part-time
Size of facility: Office 700 sq. ft.; Manufacturing 3,300 sq ft.; Warehouse 2,400 sq ft.
Lease length: 6 years remaining + (2) 4 year options to renew at market rates
Hours of operation: Mon - Thur: 6:30 am to 4:00 pm, Fri: 6:30 am to 12 noon.

Financial Performance:

Year to Date (07/1/04-09/30/04)	P&L	Fiscal Year Ended 06/30/04	P&L	Fiscal Year Ended 6/30/03	P&L
Total Revenues	$ 173,672	Total Revenues	$ 637,326	Total Revenues	$ 586,977
Cost of sales	78,658	Cost of Sales	271,983	Cost of Sales	268,524
Gross Profit	95,014	Gross Profit	365,343	Gross Profit	318,453
Overhead	74,303	Overhead	293,962	Overhead	252,505
Net Income	20,711	Net Income	71,381	Net Income	65,948
Seller Add Backs	14,560	Seller Add Backs	54,379	Seller Add Backs	47,854
Total Adjusted Net Income	$ 35,271	Total Adjusted Net Income	$ 125,760	Total Adjusted Net Income	$ 113,802

(Note: A second page can be used to review asking price, terms, allocation of purchase price and other facts about the offering.)

CHAPTER NINE

ADVICE FOR BUYERS ON LOCATING A BUSINESS

It was noted earlier that the process of locating a business you want to buy is quite similar to what you'd do when hunting for satisfactory employment. There are traditional sources to explore in electronic and print classified ads, advisors to work with, and the more resourceful techniques, such as cold calling on targets of interest.

And, just as with a job search, there is no "best" way to find a suitable business. You are advised to do a little of everything, following formal and informal procedures. Be prepared for your business search to take anywhere from six months to two years – longer than most job hunts.

On-Line Listings

The chief source of listings and information about small businesses for sale – and thus the most popular traditional strategy – is the Internet, where data banks list everything from the simplest, low-investment opportunities (how about a nice shoe shine stand?) to offerings with several employees and prices that reach the maximum value for a small business – about $5 million.

One useful resource for finding opportunities is the *www.USABizMart.com* site because of the speed and easy access to so many businesses being offered – hundreds of new listings are added each week – and because of the wealth of information, ideas and other rcsourccs that are available from that site.

The site – a robust resource responsible for connecting thousands of buyers and sellers throughout the country every week – allows buyers to organize their search for available businesses according to type of business, geographic area, or by using the advanced search mode to hunt for offerings using key words. You'll also see photos accompanying featured businesses on the site.

Classified Ads in Print

Until a few years ago when the Internet took over as the prime repository of classified listings – serving scores of industries and all kinds of consumer and business interests – the chief resource for buyers was the classified ad pages of their local newspapers. Most of the metropolitan dailies throughout the U.S. carry classified ads offering businesses for sale.

And while most offerings of small businesses are posted online, you'll find some opportunities advertised only in print. The newspapers still serve buyers who don't have easy and anytime access to the Internet.

The other way to find classified ads for companies being offered is by searching in the trade magazines covering those industries which most interest you. This takes a bit more time and effort than going on-line or opening your newspaper. Still, it's a good strategy if you want to focus on a specific business that might not get promoted in other media.

A few years ago, a plumber I'm familiar with suffered a back injury and was unable to continue in the trade. He received disability insurance payments but needed more income. He had the idea to find out if there were any plumbing supply businesses for sale in his area. There were no listings on line or in the local papers for such a business, but he did find one advertised for sale in a trade periodical to which he subscribed.

The best way to pursue this strategy may be to identify a few businesses in which you have a particular interest. Then obtain the industry-specific publications that are read by those in the targeted businesses. Your public library has a directory of these periodicals you can use to find the appropriate publications.

Another place to find these publications as well as possible "for sale" notices is at the offices of the associations that represent the businesses which you'd like to target in your search efforts. There's a wealth of information to be obtained from this source. A check of the yellow pages in your telephone book under "associations," "business and trade organizations," "chambers of commerce", "women's organizations" and "labor organizations" will give you the information you need to contact dozens of these offices. And they may have their own publications, bulletin boards or even a knowledgeable person you can talk with to get information about who, in their business, wants to retire, and how to learn more about the person's company.

Residents of heavily populated areas will find enough of these organizations to stay busy for months. The pickings will be slimmer for residents in rural locations, but you can call or email these resources at their city-based offices to start a dialog and receive their newsletters and other information that can lead you to businesses being offered.

Business Brokers and Agents

If you don't find a business you like using the more traditional sources, you undoubtedly will notice some advertising from business sales professionals – brokers or agents. They not only offer an abundance of information about what's available, they can help direct you to the opportunities that make the most sense based on your interests and abilities. At least the good brokers and agents can do that. Your research among the brokers offering businesses for sale will likely take several unexpected turns, as the people you talk to may want to switch you to something other than what you contacted them about. That's all right if your broker contact understands your wants, needs and abilities, and doesn't try to persuade you to buy just something that he or she is motivated to sell.

With helpful representatives, you will have quick access to information about businesses that may be just right for you. If you draw the short straw, however, by connecting with someone – for example, as a result of your phone call in response to an ad – who is neither knowledgeable nor dedicated to client service, you may have your time wasted. We covered, in some detail in an earlier chapter, ideas about how you can find, evaluate and select the business sales professionals who can aid you the most.

Advertising for Businesses

If you are a typical entrepreneur, you won't be content to wait for the right business to appear in the classified ads. And you won't just sit at home, hoping that you'll get a call from a member of your team of business brokers and agents to alert you about a promising opportunity.

Among the proactive steps you can take is to write ads for yourself, letting prospective sellers know about your capabilities and your interest in talking to them if they're ready to sell. These ads can be placed in the same locations where you find businesses being offered, including Internet and printed classifieds. And if you would like to be notified when a specific kind of business becomes available in your area, you might be able to pay to post a notice in the office of the association that represents the target industry. Or advertise in the industry association's newsletter.

Some of the main points listed in your acquisition resume belong in your ad. And it can be worded like one of the following:

Example 1

Wanted to buy: Manufacturing business with annual sales in the range of $1 million to $10 million. Have $250,000 cash for down payment, $200,000 real estate equity, and access to additional funds for working capital. Substantial business management experience. Contact (name and contact information).

Example 2

Cash buyer has $100,000 down payment for distribution or retail business with history of steady earnings and seller willing to train. Have business experience and bank line of credit. Contact (name and contact information).

Example 3

Attention business owners ready to retire: Serious buyer for your company with as much as $125,000 in cash and bank credit. Will respect your confidentiality. Please, no franchises. Contact (name and contact information).

Example 4

Ready to buy your restaurant. Have cash and food service experience. Will consider unprofitable businesses if fairly priced with good lease. Contact (name and contact information).

Include Advisors and Vendors

And don't stop with your ad campaign. You can extend your search to the inner sanctum where the decision to sell is formulated. By contacting attorneys and accountants, you are going right to the source – the people who would be first to know about any retirement planning by business owners among their clientele. Having done this – attempting to get in with some business attorneys and CPAs – I discovered that while many of them are reluctant to take the time to sit down with someone who isn't a source of immediate business, they are willing to set up a file for your letter and contact information. And some took my calls when I phoned to remind them to tell their clients about my interests.

It took a while before I got a response using this technique, and I was disappointed about the quality of businesses offered. But the exercise demonstrated that this could be a good source of leads if a buyer continues to work with it.

And while you're at it, contact some of the vendors in your targeted businesses. They frequently learn when an owner is ready to sell. In fact, there are times when a supplier is aware that one of his or her customers needs to sell before the customer does.

An example of this was demonstrated when Sam, a recent immigrant made the rounds of the wholesale food distributors in his area to let them know he and his family wanted to own a grocery store. He provided each with a copy of his acquisition resume stating how much money he had and detailing his experience in the business.

This clever tactic was almost immediately successful. The manager for one of the packaged foods warehouses introduced Sam to an elderly man who, because of an illness, was unable to keep his convenience store open during the long hours needed to accommodate customers. The deal that resulted was a win-win-win as it allowed the seller to retire, provided the new owner with a business to work in and build up with his family, and allowed the warehouse manager to replace a poor customer with a new one who did more business and made larger purchases.

A strategy like this can apply to most any industry. The wholesale suppliers, equipment providers and business-to-business services that work with companies in your area of interest are familiar with everyone in their territory. These vendors know who is successful, who is preparing to retire, and who is doing an inadequate job of managing a business and should turn it over to more competent ownership.

Every route driver and sales person can be a potential scout for you, as each of them knows anyone in the territory who might be a suitable seller. There is no reason you can't pay a finder's fee for someone who puts you on to the right lead.

I like this approach because it makes the buyer an "insider." Have you ever learned about a good business that you might have bought, had you known it was for sale, but it went to someone "on the inside" before the seller even had a chance to offer the company to the market? The insider can be you, if you get yourself known as a serious buyer in the industry and you can show how there will be a benefit for anyone able to introduce you to the right opportunity.

A Guerrilla Campaign at the Source

Any reason you can't do what business brokers and agents do when they go on cold calling safaris? If you think you'd like to own the business where you bring your dry cleaning, pick up imported cheeses, or browse for books and magazines, and the proprietor looks like he needs a vacation, just ask if there might be an interest in selling to you. Have a copy of your acquisition resume to hand over so the business owner can give the idea some thought and contact you if interested.

Keep in mind, if you're doing this, that most business owners are fearful about their employees learning that they want to sell. That's because once the word gets out, employees may move on, and some customers may feel less loyal and start frequenting the competitor's business. So find a way to take up the subject discretely with the seller when you approach him or her about this idea.

The plan can apply to professional practices also. So if you're a dentist, an architect or a CPA, you can contact people in the industry to learn if any have an interest in retiring.

Some buyers I've worked with used sophisticated marketing methods such as mail campaigns targeted at companies they thought might be interesting. You can start implementing this strategy by conducting a little research at your local public library. Get a directory of local businesses and you'll be able to get some valuable data, including the description of the business, address and phone number information, number of employees and owner's name. Some of these resources even list annual sales and the company's credit rating.

The information is not all accurate, so don't rely on the circumstances of the target company being exactly what is reported in the directory. This means if you're putting together a target list of companies with five to ten employees, you might include those listed with 15 or 20 employees. An interesting company listed with sales of $2 million a year should probably be contacted, even if you don't think you want to target any business that doesn't reach at least $5 million in annual revenue.

What I have seen work successfully is the use of a simple postcard for the mailing. It invites the recipient to call you if interested in talking about the sale to you of his or her business. Give your contact information. You might want to add some statements that will make your "pitch" more persuasive. Point out that you will respect the business owner's request for confidentiality, that you are not a broker soliciting for listings, and that you are willing to pay a fair price for a good business.

You can follow up with phone calls to the more interesting of the prospects on your list. Speak directly to the owner and let him or her know that you understand this might not be a good time for them to speak. Ask when you can call back or if they would prefer to call you. If they are not interested, perhaps they know someone – a colleague or neighbor – in a similar business who is ready to retire. Tell the person about your finder's fee program and ask if you should send your acquisition resume.

And you can go door-to-door in industrial parks, where you'll find service as well as distribution and manufacturing businesses. I know the idea of cold calling like that makes some people feel squeamish. You can take heart in the knowledge that since you aren't calling on the business owner to sell something – in fact you want to be the customer – you might get a pleasant reception. Provide your acquisition resume and ask for referrals to other possible acquisition candidates if the person you're speaking with isn't interested.

Remember the importance of discretion. One of the business brokers who practices cold calling in search of listings knows that business owners don't want to be seen, by employees, talking to a business broker. So this broker is very careful in the way she approaches this project. She learns the names of owners from one of the local business directories, then asks for the person by name when she enters the place of business. She never reveals her business affiliation when she is greeted by the receptionist or customer service person. She explains that her visit with the owner will take only a moment and that it is a personal matter. And she says "I'm not here to sell anything."

Then if she can meet with the owner briefly, she explains who she is and how she may be able to assist. Then she tells the owner: "I realize this is not the time or place to discuss this. When would be convenient for us to meet off premises or speak privately on the phone about how I can help you sell?"

And if she is unable to get a quick, private chat with the owner – either the person is not there or refuses to give her the time – she follows with a phone call or a letter with its envelope addressed by hand and marked "confidential." She usually explains the reason for her contact in these private communications, but never leaves a message in the general voice mailbox when she phones.

The broker is quite successful at obtaining listings with this technique. Her strategy is to try a few times to contact the owner – using an unannounced visit, phone call or personal letter – at least enough so the seller knows she wants to speak with him or her and why.

"If I can't make contact with them," she says, "I take that to mean they aren't interested. But if I do hear back, they usually appreciate the professional way that I conduct myself."

A buyer interested in contacting prospective sellers of small businesses would do well to incorporate her approach.

And Some Smart Search Practices

Providing ideas about locating a suitable business to buy is not meant to give the impression the project will be easy. In fact, it's not like any other purchase, which is noted for eager sellers vying for your attention and your dollars.

It's not just the possibility of having to compete with other buyers that makes it difficult to become the owner of an existing fast food franchise, or a small plastic forming company, or whatever business you've been considering. You'll find yourself embarked on a grand campaign – a frustrating one at times – as you consider all of the offerings, rejecting the vast majority of them, and keeping alive the hope of finding one that you like and that meets your criteria.

Patience is a key requirement

As was noted earlier, the work of finding a suitable business can take six months in the best case, and more frequently, up to two years. Maybe even longer. So it might be a good idea for you to hang on to your day job – at least for now.

Many small business owners are unrealistic or uninformed – perhaps both – when they decide to sell. They manage to crowd the market with offerings that aren't well prepared to be offered to buyers. And that means you, the buyer, will be asked to look at companies with serious problems (short time remaining on the lease, a history of financial losses, a high level of uncollected receivables), and very high asking prices.

Considering that less than half of small businesses placed on the market are actually sold, chances are that less than fifty percent of the offerings presented to you might seem to have the essentials needed to be desirable to any potential buyer. And of those, only a few will represent the kind of business you want; and fewer still will meet your financial requirements.

And if, after looking at hundreds of prospective businesses, you identify a few to investigate further, you'll then discover only a handful of this much smaller population to be worth making an offer on.

That's when you'll move into the next phase of your search, this time, competing with other buyers for the few sensible offerings in your area of interest and financial needs.

A little discipline

If you've played baseball or softball, you'll understand the analogy between looking for a suitable business to buy and waiting for a pitch to come right over home plate in the middle of the strike zone. The relevant advice here is not to try to buy something out of frustration and impatience, just as the pitching coach will tell you to resist the urge to swing at anything just because you've waited in the batter's box so long and you're eager to get a hit.

Like a curve ball coming at you, a business you're considering may not be what it seems. In fact, in most cases it is not what you thought when you first learned about it.

Talking to buyers and prospective buyers is revealing for all the stories they tell about the weeks and months of meetings with prospective sellers and with business sales professionals. One buyer who finally found a distribution business he liked after more than two years of a continuous search, explains that the hardest part was forcing himself to continue looking at possibilities, knowing that each was almost certainly going to be a waste of his time. But he did it anyway and stayed on his mission.

He explains that he changed his optimistic mindset: "I finally got out of the habit of thinking 'maybe the next business opportunity I hear about will be the one for me.' I got to the point – when I'd go to see a business or meet with a broker about something – that I knew for sure I was not going to like what they had to show me. It helped me to not be so disappointed."

Be ready to move

Now that the buyer is in a properly cautious frame of mind, is convinced that most every business reviewed will be inappropriate and is afraid to "take a swing" at an offering that seems to be interesting but may turn out to be a "curve ball," I should point out that you'll never buy a business if you don't step up to the plate in the first place. You've got to make an offer on what looks appealing.

Some buyers let the horror stories about over-priced listings and buying mistakes deter them from making a move on a business opportunity, even if they like it. After repeatedly examining companies for sale that were revealed to be unsatisfactory, a buyer might (understandably) conclude that every business which seems, at first glance, to be interesting, has a fatal flaw. It's just a matter of discovering what the problem is.

But if a business stands up to the initial investigation: If the revenues appear to be there, the reputation is sound, the future seems promising, the premises pass inspection and the price and terms appear within reason, it's imperative that you put in your bid. Remember that you still can refuse to move forward on the transaction if your due diligence reveals problems with the company that you didn't see at first.

You may not get to see very many good businesses that meet your criteria, but if you look long enough, you will see a few. When it appears you've discovered that unique situation, don't neglect to put in an offer to buy it.

Selling yourself to the seller

An interesting finding that I've repeatedly confirmed in my conversations with sellers over the years is that even though their main priority, initially, was to get the most money possible under the best terms, at least half admit their final decisions had more to do with the quality of the buyer than the size of the deal.

The factor that persuaded many to enter into a deal, even at a price and terms that didn't quite meet what they were asking, was simply that they liked the buyer and felt the person would be successful in the business.

As noted in an earlier chapter, the buyer's success in the business directly impacts the seller, particularly when there is seller financing involved. And there may also be a psychological reason to explain why sellers sometimes – incredibly – put personality ahead of profits. The buyer who respects what the seller has accomplished with the business, and who shows enthusiasm for the ideas and systems the seller has put in place over the years, will probably make that seller feel pretty good about himself or herself. And that feeling is quite likely to help the seller become favorably disposed to the buyer's bid to purchase the business.

I'm not advocating that you pour so much praise on the other person that they need to "get out the shovel," but that you acknowledge the good work the seller has accomplished – after all, this is one of the few businesses you might want! And make it clear that you are open to the seller's ideas for insuring the company's continued success.

As is often the case, yours might be one of two, or even of three proposals being considered by the seller. If you are the seller's favorite prospect, it will help decide in your favor, in the event other offers are close to yours in price and terms. And even if your bid is too low, the seller may want to counter offer your proposal with the price at which he or she is willing to sell, and give you the option of getting first in line to buy by saying yes to the counter offer.

Part of that respect for the seller is demonstrated by recognizing and observing the conditions of showing that the seller has requested. I hear of too many instances where a buyer violates the non-disclosure and privacy pact to which he or she agrees as a condition of learning about a business. It is not all right to discuss the business owners' intention to sell with employees, vendors, customers, or with anyone else for that matter. Even if the seller claims to have revealed the truth about the sale, it is not the buyer's job to let the information out. That's up to the seller.

Even with an accepted offer, unless you have the express permission of the business owner to take it up with certain parties (such as the company's vendors and customers), there is no justification for you to discuss the impending sale with anyone except your advisors. Violating the non-disclosure requirement is probably the quickest way to alienate the seller and lose the deal. And you may have additional problems if the seller wants to hold you liable for some loss suffered because of something you revealed that should have been kept quiet.

Conclusion

Finding a small business for you to buy can be a challenge, not unlike finding the right job, although locating a suitable business will likely require more time than it takes to land a good job.

There are various strategies that can be employed to uncover a willing seller of a suitable company, and the prospective buyer is advised to consider all of them, and use as many as possible so as to have several things working at once. These strategies include the simplest, which is accessing business-for-sale want ads on the Internet and in print, to the most guerrilla-like methods of cold calling and advertising for businesses to buy.

Business brokers and agents can be an excellent resource. Another suggestion is to cold call on businesses and speak to the owners. This can be productive, but is a strategy that must be handled carefully so that employees and customers don't catch on to what you're doing. A few tips offered by someone successful at this technique are included to help you use this approach successfully.

Smart search practices include being patient, as it may take from 6 months to 2 years before you find the right business. And it's important to be disciplined, so you don't run out of patience and buy a company that is not right, just because you fear having no business to show for your many months of trying to find one. When you discover a business that does seem right, waste no time in making an offer. Even if it doesn't meet the seller's requirements, if you get a counter offer, at least you've got things moving forward on a company you think you'd like to own. You also are advised to sell yourself to the seller, beginning with the day of your first meeting. This can help to persuade the other party to work with you if you want to buy their business.

KEY POINTS FROM THIS CHAPTER

❖ *Finding a business can be compared to the hunt for a job in terms of the fact that there are several ways to go about it, and the best strategy is to employ as many means as possible.*

❖ *The most common method of locating businesses for sale is the researching of on-line listings. Among the most widely used Internet resources for small businesses for sale is www.USABizMart.com, which is responsible for matching thousands of buyers and sellers every month.*

❖ *Before on-line sources were available, the number one destination for people investigating businesses for sale was the listings that appeared in newspaper classified advertising sections. These still can help you uncover some offerings which may not be posted on line. And printed classifieds provide a resource for those who don't have ready access to the Internet.*

❖ *Printed classifieds also can be found in trade periodicals and are recommended for those who want to research available businesses in targeted industries. Your public library has directories in which you can find industry-specific publications for this purpose.*

❖ *Business brokers and agents – if you work with ones who are competent – are a very good source of information about businesses for sale, and can help you to negotiate for, and to purchase a company that you want to own.*

❖ *Among the more pro-active techniques is to run your own "business wanted" ads in an on-line service or in a trade periodical that focuses on an industry which you want to target.*

❖ *Vendors are an excellent source of information regarding whom, among their customers, may want to sell. Someone providing goods or services to other businesses usually knows a great deal about those enterprises, how successful they are, and whether the current owner would benefit by selling out.*

❖ *Business advisors, such as attorneys and accountants, are the first people to know when the business owners among their clients want to retire or sell for other reasons. Providing your acquisition resume to these professionals is another possible way to uncover a good business for sale.*

❖ *Consider offering a finder's fee to someone who can direct you to a seller whose business you purchase.*

❖ Also recommended as a pro-active method is launching a mail campaign to business owners, explaining your interest in learning if they want to sell.

❖ This same approach, but conducted in person, can be effective if handled in such a way as to respect a seller's concern for confidentiality. Don't tell the receptionist who greets you that you want to buy the business, only that you have a "brief and personal" matter to discuss with the owner.

❖ Considering that less than half of small businesses on the market ever sell, it's most likely that many opportunities you'll be exposed to are not in a condition to be marketable. From that short list of possibilities, you'll reject most offerings, as they will not be of interest to you, or not in your price range.

❖ It's necessary for a person wanting to purchase a small business to be very patient. Your hunt will go on for a long time and may subject you to a number of hopeful moments – when you think you've discovered a suitable business – that are followed by disappointment, when you discover the enterprise is not as appealing as it first seemed.

❖ Another search practice to adopt is one of discipline. I've seen buyers become so frustrated at the long months of effort with no results that they finally purchase a business that is not what they want, just so they can get on with managing a company and put an end to the "business shopping."

❖ It's not uncommon to be frustrated in the search, particularly when you see businesses you like, only to learn they aren't as profitable as you'd thought, and will require more working capital than you'd anticipated.

❖ Another frustration comes about when a buyer finally discovers a suitable business, only to lose out to someone else who saw it first, or who offered the seller a better deal.

❖ Selling yourself to the seller is an important and useful strategy if you want your offer to be carefully considered and if you want to look forward to his or her cooperation throughout the negotiating process and beyond.

❖ Your observance of the non-disclosure agreement will help you maintain a solid relationship with the seller and keep you out of trouble.

CHAPTER TEN

EVALUATING CANDIDATES

If the seller's most important task is preparation, both of your company and your selling package, the next most important thing you can do when offering your small business for sale is to be sure that you are working only with buyer prospects who are qualified to do business with you.

Similarly, a critical responsibility for prospective buyers is to verify that businesses you may be considering are worth your time and attention.

Perhaps these requirements seem so obvious that they need not be mentioned. Yet it actually is quite easy for small business owners to get so caught up in the selling process – answering questions, conducting tours of the facility, providing information – that you neglect to verify that the prospect you're working with actually has the ability to move forward on a purchase of your business if, in fact, he or she wants to do so. And buyers can easily spend countless hours inquiring about a business and meeting with brokers, owners and owner representatives without having seen any documentation to verify the statements being made.

Since your time is too valuable to waste with people and with offerings that are not qualified – people who may want to do business with you, but don't have what it takes to meet your criteria – it's important that buyers and sellers remain aware of the possibility of this happening. And be prepared to move away quickly if you discover that your wishful thinking – your hopes for a solid buyer, your expectations of a really great business offering – has compelled you to waste time and energy on a target of interest that really does not merit your attention.

And by limiting time wasting investigations, you're likely to find that the frustration level starts to decline. If the somewhat cynical attitude noted earlier becomes the companion of the business buyer, he or she will be less patient when the requested information about a business offering is not forthcoming. Rather than waiting hopefully for proof of the earnings you were told about in connection with a business that looks interesting, and starting to imagine yourself in control of the company, you'll focus your energy on the effort to uncover more business possibilities. It's to your benefit to adopt the notion that the more situations you are aware of, the more likely you'll be to find the right business opportunity. And, in the meantime, it might be useful to assume the point of view, as expressed by one buyer: "I'll believe it when I see it."

A rather hard line is also recommended for sellers. Of course you want to accommodate people who express an interest in what you have to offer. But if it is difficult to coax the information you need from someone who's inquiring about your offering, you need to make your requirements clear and insist they be followed.

Yes, you do risk chasing away a good, qualified buyer by insisting on getting answers to your questions before the person is ready to share. But it's worth the risk so as to avoid the wasted time and the frustration that come from trying to make a sale to someone who can't buy.

Seller Qualifies Buyer Prospects

It's useful for sellers, whether or not you are experienced at qualifying prospective customers in your business, to take a lesson from skilled business brokers who are good at managing this step in the process. One broker describes the art of qualifying buyers as "walking the tightrope."

"If you push too hard for information," he explains, "the prospect can feel boxed in and surrounded. The only escape is to run from you. And if that was a good buyer who got away, well, you just lost."

But the alternative, he points out, is to fail to ask the important questions early in the conversation: "If you don't learn what you need to know, you might find out you're just being led down the garden path. There are plenty of sweet sentiments along your way. But no sale. It's another way to lose."

This broker recommends adopting a helpful attitude, with a willingness to answer questions and do what you can to let people learn what you have to offer. But then temper your helpfulness with an insistence on getting the cooperation of the other party.

He says: "It's fine to treat a prospective buyer for your business the way you do the customers who you deal with on a daily basis. They get your attention; your energy is there to provide service.

"But don't cross the line on the side of being overly accommodating without expecting some consideration in return."

Another broker explains that good sales people in most any industry attempt to – in her words – "orchestrate the interaction as much as possible.

"You can't really control another person," she says. "In fact, that's not something you want to do. It's not healthy for people to relate to each other that way. And it's not good business."

She continues: "But you do want to take the initiative, if you can. You can set the agenda and make sure your objectives are clearly on the table. You get more accomplished that way, than if you just shake hands with the prospective buyer and talk about the weather to break the ice and then hope for the best."

Here are example conversation openers that will give you ideas about setting the tone in a meeting with a prospective buyer, so that the dance referred to in the previous chapter is at least conducted according to your rhythm. Consider these ideas and think about how you can adapt one or more of these approaches to your style and personality.

Sample Approaches

Example One

I think it would use your time efficiently, and also mine, if we exchange some information. Then you can consider whether you are interested in investigating my business further and I can evaluate whether I think you'd make a suitable buyer.

I'd like to go over the basic information about the business and I have a package to give you to study so you can determine if you might want to buy the business. At the same time, I want to know more about you, I am interested in learning the same kind of information about you that I'm giving you about the business.

I'd like to understand a bit about your background, and I want to know about your financial situation: how much cash you have to work with and if you have arranged for added financing to help you make a purchase. I also want to know if you have good credit. That's in case we agree on a deal for the business that includes me carrying back some of the purchase price with a promissory note.

Does this seem fair?

I have a non-disclosure form here for you to agree to. And if you want me to acknowledge in writing that I will not share any information about your personal and financial situation except with my business advisors, I'll be glad to do that.

(This example form is available at *www.USABizMart.com* Select "Tools" page and find Non-Disclosure & Confidentiality Agreement.)

Example Two

When we spoke and I sent you a (blind) profile on the business, I also included a non-disclosure form. I'd like to get that back from you with your approval of it (signed). I'll put the name of my business on it and then we can proceed with me giving you more information about the business and answering your questions.

Did you bring the form? If not, I have another one here. I'm sure you understand how important it is that the information I'm about to give you is treated with the strictest confidentiality.

I also sent you a blank financial statement form. Did you get a chance to complete that? I'm willing to disclose to you some very private data about my business. It's important you know these things so that you can decide if this business is for you. At the same time, I think it's only fair that I understand about your background and financial ability. And I will treat any information you give me with the same respect for confidentiality that you treat the information I give you.

If you didn't bring your financial statement I have another blank here. I realize you don't have your personal records with you so you may not have all the details at your disposal. But just fill it out to the best of your ability, and please put your signature at the bottom. I'll give you a few minutes to go ahead and do that, and then we can talk about the business.

Example Three

As you can probably imagine, I have had a number of calls in response to my advertising. The fact is, there just are not that many good businesses available and at reasonable terms. So a lot of people have contacted me and are interested in learning more.

I'm pleased to answer all of your questions as well as I can, and to give you as much information as you need, so you can decide if this business is of interest. And in order to do that, I just need to verify that you are one of the people I've heard from who would be a suitable buyer – if you're interested.

So if you can answer a few questions for me, that'll help us move forward in this process.

Okay?

In the interests of respecting your time, and mine, I put a couple of forms in the mail to you – a non-disclosure agreement and a financial statement. Why don't we start with those?

These ideas originate from experienced sales professionals who understand that no one solution is applicable to every situation. And that some situations – and some people – can be particularly difficult to manage.

Certainly you're correct if you've concluded that prospective buyers for your business aren't likely to fall in line with everything you suggest at every occasion. The intent in offering these phrases (in show business they would be called "opening lines") is not to give you all the tools you need to dominate the conversation. That's not realistic. But they will have served their purpose if they provoke some ideas about how you might take the initiative and press for your objectives in meetings with prospective buyers.

The point of view I'd like to share with you is a perspective meant for sellers who have difficulty walking that tightrope mentioned a bit earlier. If your habit is to give customers the upper hand in negotiations or in disputes, the concept for you to take away from these paragraphs is that any prospective buyers for your business owe you as much respect as you owe them. They need to be willing to accommodate your needs – for confidentiality and for facts about their qualifications – if you are to be expected to answer their questions and provide the information they request.

And for sellers who are quick to assume that your buyer candidates should be dismissed, disregarded and distrusted – until they prove otherwise – these brief samples of dialogue are meant to demonstrate another approach you can take. If you can use it to get a prospect to participate in the dance, you can move forward in the process of mutual discovery, without the fear that you are giving everything away for free.

In either event, sellers are encouraged to think about these suggested approaches and consider how you might modify them so they are consistent with the way you work and communicate with others.

Some Questions to Ask

I know brokers who have a list of qualifying questions and when they ask the prospective buyers for information they merely go down the page, from 1 through 25, recording every answer. It's good that they're careful not to miss anything when qualifying prospective buyers, but I like to be a little more spontaneous than that when talking to another person. It's also good to build a rapport. And that's easier to do when your interaction is more like conversation rather than taking a poll. Whatever your style, here are some questions for which you should have answers from prospective buyers who want to move forward and learn about your business.

First the questions calling for definitive answers – what I consider the quantitative evaluation. Note that this is the kind of questioning you can use to give your buyer a passing or failing grade. And the "right" answers are provided.

- Have you been looking for a business for awhile? (If less than six months, the prospect is still on the steep learning curve as to what's available and may not have a realistic picture of the market. If more than two years, be aware that this may be a perfectionist unlikely to find anything to buy without changing his/her requirements.)

- Do you know the kind of business you're looking for? (A "yes or "I have a general idea" is the answer you want. If the person claims to be "open to anything" it's most likely a sign of a buyer still not focused, and consequently, more difficult to deal with.)

- Have you owned a business before? (Many serious and qualified buyers have not yet taken the plunge so the lack of this background should not be reason to shut them out of contention. But someone who has been an owner is more likely to speak your language.)

- Have you got experience managing people? (If you have employees, it's best to get a "yes" to this question. Buyers without this experience may be in over their heads trying to run your company.)

- Have you made an offer on a business before? (The "yes" answer here tells you that your prospect is probably serious. Besides, having been involved in one or more prior offers, the prospect is likely to be gaining an education in the realities of the market.)

- How much cash do you have to work with? (The right answer is, of course, whatever is the amount of cash necessary to make the down payment on your offering and still have enough remaining for working capital.)

- Have you made arrangements to get financing to help with a purchase? (The prospect should get double points for a "yes" answer. It demonstrates the prospect is serious and is planning ahead. It also means the person may be able to get the funds needed to take over your business.

- Do you understand why it's so important to me to keep this process confidential? (Expect a "yes" answer and be worried if you don't get it. One reason to ask the question is to remind the prospect of how critical it is to you that the proprietary information you're sharing is not disclosed to others.)

- Have you got good credit? (Naturally, a prospect with a perfect credit history is preferable to one whose credit report sinks like the Titanic. But a business buyer with a less than pristine credit record may have a good explanation and should be given the benefit of the doubt. At least the answer "not perfect" is probably an honest one. The "wrong" answer involves the appearance of evasiveness – the person seems reluctant to discuss this subject and, perhaps, avoids eye contact.)

Mixed in with these, should be a few qualitative questions. These are more open-ended, calling for some description on the part of the person being qualified. A good way to interpret these answers is to look at body language and try to guess what's on the buyer's mind as well as what comes out of his or her mouth. And depending on the answers, and the impression you get of the person while he or she is answering, you may decide to alter the "score" they got when responding to the questions of the first type.

A few suggested qualitative questions are:

If you've made offers on another business – or other businesses – what happened? Did you make a purchase? If not, why not?

Why do you want to own your own business?

Tell me something about your working background?

Do you want to be a passive owner or do you expect to be active in your business?

These questions – both the quantitative and qualitative questions – are among the most important ones to ask. And reviewing this list will probably help you to come up with others to pose to a prospective buyer who is looking at your small business.

How to Make the Most of Your Meeting with Buyer Prospects

Speaking of asking questions, if you've given any thought to this process while reading about it, you may have questions of your own about how to successfully conduct the qualifying of buyer prospects. Here are a few insights.

Be clear about your objective

During your initial meeting with a prospective buyer, it's very helpful to keep in mind exactly what you are trying to achieve. Don't be a business owner who thinks the sale has to be made at the first session. That agenda will confuse you and frighten the buyer.

Instead, the three useful things to accomplish at this point are: 1. Give the buyer enough information about the business so that he or she can determine if interested. That should be easy to do if you have a well-prepared package to hand over. You can quickly review the material and answer any questions to complete the presentation. 2. Find out if the – buyer is qualified to buy your business. The answers to your qualifying questions will give you some useful clues if you don't know for sure. And remember to take the pulse of your instincts. Ask yourself if this person is someone with whom you can do business, and someone who's likely to be successful as owner of your enterprise. 3. Set the stage for what comes next. It's a mistake to leave things up in the air. You don't want the prospective buyer to "get back to you when I get a chance." Agree on a date – at least two days and no more than a week forward – to speak again about whether the buyer wants to tour the facility and get more information. Your prospect needs, and should have a few days to digest the information and determine if your business warrants further investigation. But don't leave it open ended.

I've learned that delays are like a deadly disease that kills deals. Instill a sense of urgency in your buyers, making sure they understand it's important to you for discussions and negotiations – if they're going to take place – to keep moving forward at a steady pace.

Non-disclosure/Confidentiality Agreement

By signing this form, the buyer prospect promises that whatever he or she learns about your business, including the fact that it is for sale, as a result of the interaction with you, will not be disclosed to any party besides the buyer's immediate advisors. There is some question in the legal community about the enforceability of the non-disclosure contract. Regardless, some form of confidentiality agreement is used in nearly all introductions by business brokers and agents in most every part of the country. For the most part it is considered a useful tool for "at least" putting the buyer on notice about the seller's requirements regarding confidentiality. In extreme examples of violation of this agreement, a buyer may be liable to the seller for any damages incurred by the seller because of the buyer's actions.

Sellers are advised to decline giving information to prospective buyers without first obtaining a signature on the non-disclosure document. While a small percentage of buyer's refuse when asked to do so – usually trying to get an upper hand in the event of later negotiations – most prospective purchasers for small businesses are willing to comply with this request.

Is he or she telling the truth?

Once you obtain the non-disclosure promise, it's very useful to get a financial statement. And it doesn't hurt to ask the buyer to obtain a letter from an officer at his or her bank that confirms the buyer's representations to you about cash on hand and assets. Someone reluctant to be forthcoming with the facts you require, or unwilling to provide some proof to back up claims, may have something to hide. Repeating what I noted a little earlier in this chapter: If you have furnished the prospect with details about the business, or are about to do so, you have every right to expect the person to disclose the details of their background and their financial ability, as it pertains to the purchase of your business. If they don't want to cooperate, I feel they've proved themselves unqualified to buy your business.

If the person appears to be telling the truth, but is not, you will find out about it eventually – you hope sooner rather than later. I'm a strong advocate for taking back-up offers, even if you have a ratified contract with a buyer who is conducting a due diligence examination.

One reason to encourage back-up offers, even when you are in contract with someone who is now conducting due diligence examination, is to keep the "working" buyer moving forward. And make sure the buyer understands that you intend to have alternative buyers to work with if he or she proves unable to complete the deal as agreed. One strategy of buyers who don't provide accurate details about their financial ability, involves getting you to renegotiate the deal in their favor, once it is discovered they haven't the ability to perform according to the agreement. If such a buyer knows you're prepared to sell to someone else, if necessary, it may discourage this kind of dishonesty.

Keep your notes/folders up to date

Remember the file mentioned in a previous chapter – the one with information pertaining to the sale of your small business? Make sure the buyer folder is current so that you can refer to facts given to you by prospective buyers in case there is a discrepancy. And in this or an adjacent folder, you should have names and contact information for other buyers to stay in touch with in the event the "working" deal begins to go bad – either because the buyer doesn't want to move forward or because you learn the person was less than honest at the point where you were qualifying buyers.

What if the Buyer Doesn't Appear Qualified?

Do you know how to say "no?" Whether your tendency is to be diplomatic or blunt, it is important that you cut off discussion as soon as possible, after you've satisfied yourself that this prospect is not the buyer you want for your business. Perhaps you've reached this conclusion because you can't get agreement on signing the non-disclosure document. Maybe the person is unable or unwilling to give you satisfactory financial information, or the information provided reveals their inability to handle the purchase. And it may be your gut reaction that tells you that time spent with the person will be wasted.

In any event, remember that you are a buyer also. You have to "buy" this buyer candidate as the one you might have a deal with – the individual who might replace you as owner of your business. The buyer has a right to decline to proceed if he or she doesn't want to buy your business. And you have the same right, if you don't consider the person qualified.

If your answer to the prospect is "no," make that clear as soon as possible. Then move on to the next prospect.

Buyer Sizing up Business Offerings

The idea of being introduced by a cousin or friend to the perfect business, then working out a negotiation that allows you to become the owner in a short period of time, is a very appealing. It doesn't happen very often. Most of the time the buyer needs to behave like the director of Broadway musicals as portrayed in the movies. That's the person who has a room full of hopeful starlets who take turns auditioning for him. In most cases he gives each a minute or less, then calls out "next" to keep the process going so he can be on time for his lunch meeting with the producer at the New York-style deli.

To make your job easier, and thus somewhat less painful and frustrating, you might want to consider working with a checklist that helps flush out any problems there may be with an offering.

Yes, I'm advocating that you learn to become somewhat cynical as a buyer. It's probably the best way to keep from getting personally engaged with offerings that get your hopes up before you discover they lack promise.

I think it's the exhilaration of believing you've discovered a good business, followed by the disappointment when you find almost always, that it's not as interesting as you'd anticipated – the whole roller coaster ride of ups and downs – that makes it so difficult to be a business buyer. Try the more distant, unconcerned approach, to see if it helps you remain a little less involved and a little less frustrated by the outcomes.

Your Checklist

And whether the checklist is in your head, entered into your PDA or scrawled onto a sheet of paper in your business file, it should contain these items:

- Were financials supplied quickly?

- Did you get P&Ls and balance sheets?

- Are the financials current (up to within the past three months)?

- Does the financial information cover at least three years?

- Does the information in the financials match with the verbal statements about earnings and income made by the seller or seller's representative?

- Have the gross sales increased each year?

- What about profits?

- Can you determine total adjusted net earnings (ANE) from the P&L information provided?

- Has the ratio of ANE to gross sales increased, decreased or remained the same over the past three years?

- Has there been a substantial (more than 10%) change (up or down) in the ratio of ANE to gross sales over the last three years?

- If so, has the seller or seller's representative offered an explanation (positive or negative) for the change?

- Do receivables equal more than 60 - 75 days of sales?

- Assuming you were to meet the seller's request of price, down payment and terms, is there enough net income to meet the financing terms proposed?

- After meeting financing requirements, how much money will be left over for the compensation you receive as investor, owner and chief employee of the business?

- Did you get a copy of the premises lease?

- Do the terms stated in the lease correspond to the lease information you were given by the seller or seller's representative?

- Are there at least three years (and preferably five years) remaining on the lease?

- Are there options to renew at market rate?

- What is the ratio of rent to gross revenues?

- Has this ratio changed (plus or minus) over the past three years? If the rent is scheduled for increase in the upcoming years, how much more revenue will the business need to generate in order for the ratio of rent to gross sales to remain the same?

- Did you receive a list of capital assets?

- Does the information on these documents match what you were told by the seller or seller's representative?

- Does the equipment list include, for each item, date of acquisition, useful life, depreciated value, market value? If not, can you get this information?

- What equipment will need to be replaced in the next 12 months? What about equipment that will need replacement in the next 24 months?

- Have you asked the seller if he or she knows of any factors likely to impact the gross revenues or the profits of the business in the near future? What was the answer?

These are just preliminary matters for you to review as you begin your evaluation of a business that might make a good acquisition. Make sure that if you don't have all the information you need to begin a careful analysis of the business, that the seller or seller's representative is prepared to provide you the additional data requested.

Conclusion

The intent in this chapter is to offer some insight into the process of qualifying prospective buyers for your small business, and to provide some ideas about how to handle this important step. Without qualified buyers to work with, your efforts to sell your business are wasted. And unless buyers are correctly qualified as to work background and financial ability, there is no way to determine with certainty if anyone in the audience for whom you are presenting your business, has the capacity to join you in a transaction. As difficult as it might be for some sellers to qualify buyers before working with them, and to say "no" to those who don't qualify, it is absolutely critical that these steps are followed carefully if an owner is to achieve a successful sale of his or her business.

The smart and successful buyer will develop search criteria and evaluate any prospective business offering against those standards. And by insisting that any business opportunity of interest meet the minimum standards, the buyer will eliminate a number of sub-standard offerings for sale, thereby saving time and effort that should be focused on finding more promising enterprises.

KEY POINTS FROM THIS CHAPTER

❖ *Properly qualifying prospective buyers is among the most important things a seller can do in the process of marketing a small business.*

❖ *Verifying the suitability of a business for sale – determining if it is worth investigating – is a critical responsibility for a buyer.*

❖ *One broker describes the art of qualifying buyers as "walking the tightrope." Pushing too hard for information can chase a buyer away, while neglecting to get the information you need can result in wasting a lot of time with unqualified people.*

❖ *Another broker recommends that a seller meeting with a prospective buyer should attempt to "orchestrate the interaction as much as possible." That is done by taking the initiative and setting the agenda.*

❖ *Suggested approaches a seller can take to gain some control in a buyer qualifying meeting include: "I think it would use your time efficiently if we exchange information," "I'm willing to disclose information to you...at the same time I think it's only fair that I understand about your background and financial ability," and "I'm pleased to answer all of your questions...just need to verify you're one of the people who would be a suitable buyer. "*

❖ *Sellers who are so accustomed to providing service to customers that they're reluctant to demand financial and other personal information, should understand that buyers need to be just as accommodating as sellers are in the disclosure of information.*

❖ *Some qualifying questions to ask buyers are quantitative, requiring definitive answers. Questions of a more qualitative nature give further insight into the buyer's probable ability to complete a deal.*

❖ *Don't attempt to make a sale on an initial meeting with a buyer. Rather, the time is well spent if you can: 1. Provide the buyer with complete information about your business, 2. Find out if the buyer is qualified, and 3. Set the stage for follow up, with a definite date to further discuss the buyer's interest.*

❖ *Written information from a buyer, such as financial statement and banker letter, can help add credibility to a buyer's verbal assertions. Sellers are encouraged to obtain it.*

❖ *The Buyer's signature on a Non-disclosure/Confidentiality Agreement, early in the process, helps to prevent "leaks" of proprietary information about the seller's business, and puts the buyers on notice that he or she will be required to maintain confidentiality during (and after) investigation of the offering. At this web address: www.USABizMart.com you can obtain and download a Non-disclosure/Confidentiality Agreement form at the "Forms" section within the "Tools" tab.*

❖ *It's important for a seller to keep a file in which you maintain buyer information and also names and contact data for other buyers who might be willing to make back-up offers. An accepted back-up offer puts a person in position to buy the business if the buyer on contract with the seller is unable or unwilling to complete the transaction. Encouraging back ups is a good strategy to keep the buyer on contract moving forward.*

❖ *To avoid the frustration of not being able to find a suitable business, or learning an interesting business does not measure up to its promotion, it's recommended that buyers try not to get emotionally involved or hopeful about individual possibilities, but to believe in the process.*

❖ *A listing of some basic things to check when examining a business is offered to help the buyer focus on the most critical aspects of a business to buy.*

❖ *Delays kill deals. Make sure all buyer prospects understand that you consider it important for discussions and negotiations to move forward at a steady pace.*

❖ *When encountering buyers who aren't qualified, it helps if you know how to say "no." Whether your style is diplomatic or blunt, cut off discussion with the wrong buyer as soon as possible, so you can be free to deal with qualified buyers.*

CHAPTER ELEVEN

THE OFFER

At some point in discussions between the buyer and seller of a small business, when parties are ready to start putting together an agreement for transfer of the company, it's customary for the buyer to make an offer to purchase the business, and to present the offer, or have it presented to the seller by a broker or other representative.

The offer will be accompanied by a deposit check made out to an escrow holder or an attorney who can handle the closing of the transaction. The amount can be a flat sum of say $1,000, $5,000 or $10,000, or the amount can be a percentage of the sale price offered – such as $2,000 put down with a $200,000 offer.

Letter of Intent

An alternative to the offer is a Letter of Intent (LOI), which is commonly used for larger ($500,000 and up) and more complicated transactions. The LOI is rarely binding on the buyer unless it specifically states that acceptance on the part of the seller will obligate them both to perform. The purpose of the LOI is to establish the basic components of what will be the transaction, and determine if buyer and seller are in agreement on the terms of a deal, before they move forward with preparation of a purchase contract. It's the first draft of an agreement, stating the intention of the parties to have a deal as outlined.

If you are a buyer ready to start negotiating for a specific company, the LOI might be an appropriate document to use as your first written expression of interest in making the acquisition through purchase of the corporate stock. And the LOI procedure, followed by an attorney-written contract, is the solution if there will be complex issues or several conditions – examples are an extended escrow, the required approval of other buyers, a drawn-out due diligence period – that are too involved to be adequately covered with the standard purchase form.

In other words, if your attorney will be asked to prepare the actual agreement, it will be based on principles and language derived from your LOI to the seller.

The Offer Includes

In most cases, however, you'll probably use a standard offer form. And they are easy to acquire at, for example, *www.USABizMart.com*, where you would click on the "Tools" button to get a form you can use.

An offer form is used for most transactions involving small businesses. And once approved, it becomes the purchase agreement, as it spells out all the terms by which the parties agree to transact business. And whether using a Letter of Intent or a standard offer, you will include the same basic provisions. They are:

- Identity of parties (buyer and seller)

- Name and address of the subject business

- Sales price

- Cash down payment

- Buyer's assumption of obligations

- Terms of payment of balance due to seller

- Assets included

- Assets not included

- Seller agreements: including covenant not to compete and training

- Buyer agreements: including non-disclosure

- Method of handling such matters as inventory, payables, receivables, deposits

- Contingencies: including approvals of third parties, such as landlord, franchisor, lenders and creditors of the seller

- Buyer due diligence

- Seller due diligence

- Time considerations/deadlines

- Name of escrow company or attorney

- Determination of who will pay for escrow (usually: 50/50)

- List of items to be completed in escrow and documents to be prepared by escrow service

- Payment of fees to broker(s)

- Representations and warranties

- Legal language including provisions about treatment of deposit, consequences of breach, procedure in the event of disputes (court or arbitration?)

To make your offer more persuasive, it's a good idea to present it with a copy of your resume, your financial statement and credit report. And if you're planning to borrow extra funds, you can include a letter from the lender, stating that you are pre-approved for a loan of a certain sum to aid in the purchase of a business, subject to the lender's satisfactory review of the deal.

The seller should be granted a specific amount of time, usually two to four days, to respond, either by signing the offer as is, which makes it a contract, or by preparing a counter offer. In that event the seller usually will sign under the phrase "subject to counteroffer dated (date is specified)." That places the ball back in your court. You will have a few days to accept the agreement, as changed by the seller's counter offer, or to agree, but subject to your own counter offer.

The exchange of counteroffers, if that continues, can get a little unwieldy and confusing. You or the seller may forget where you stand with respect to various issues if you keep sending the agreement back and forth with more revisions.

The recommended procedure, after the third or fourth counteroffer has been made, and if it appears you both want to try and come to a mutual agreement, is to meet and negotiate each of the items that need to be resolved. And it's best to have a skilled negotiator, perhaps your broker or the one representing the seller, to assist in the work of reaching an understanding acceptable to both.

You'll get a chance to learn a bit about negotiations in a following chapter.

What is Getting Sold

You probably know that two honest, well meaning people can look at the same situation and come away with different ideas about it. That's why it's a good idea for you to be thorough and explicit in describing what you expect to be included in the business that you propose to buy. You probably will want:

Business name and trade style

It's surprising how many purchase contracts neglect to mention that the name of the business and its trade style, or logo, are included in the deal and should belong to the buyer when he or she takes over. That goes for the phone number as well. It may be understood that these are part of the goodwill, but it doesn't hurt to make the intention clear. I'm familiar with transactions that stumbled over what should be this obvious factor. In one case the seller announced that he was planning to open a day care facility for dogs in another city under the same trade name. His new enterprise would be far enough away from the business he was selling that there would be no violation of his covenant not to compete. But he claimed that if the buyer operated under his name and earned a bad reputation with poor service, it would reflect negatively on the seller's new business. He told the buyer that she could have all the other assets of the business, but not the business' name. This disclosure came at the very last minute, but the buyer declined to proceed with the transaction under those circumstances. Much time and unrefundable escrow and due diligence expenses were spent unnecessarily. The disagreement would have been confronted at the beginning of the negotiations had the buyer's intent to use the trade name been specifically stated in the offer.

Hard assets

In the category of hard assets you'll find all of the equipment used in the business, as well as the furniture, fixtures and even supplies. For a manufacturing company, or a processing business, such as a machine shop, and for certain kinds of service providers – including everything from a shoe repair shop to a hi-tech medical imaging clinic – the equipment is vital to the conduct of the business. This is even true in some service businesses where the only valuable asset is software used to manage customer accounts. The best way to be specific about what you expect to have included among the hard assets is to attach a list of everything as an exhibit or an addendum to the agreement. The list may be the one provided to you by the seller as part of the offering package. If that list is not complete, the offer should spell out the requirement that it be completed, and its contents agreed on, within a specified number of days following acceptance of the offer.

This also is the approach to take if no list exists, and you haven't had the opportunity to compile it – perhaps because you haven't been at the premises long enough to scrutinize everything in detail.

I'm reminded of a deal on a Toyota repair garage that almost wound up in court over a fight regarding the computer disks containing repair manuals. The seller maintained they were his personal property, and he needed them for reference when repairing his own car. The buyer felt that they were part of the equipment of the shop, needed for proper conduct of the business, and that the seller had no right to keep them. Besides that, they were very expensive to replace. The matter was finally resolved in favor of the buyer, but not before each party spent several hundred dollars in attorney fees.

And while it isn't necessary to count paper clips and spare rolls of toilet paper, I have seen lists that included items such as telephone, clock, waste basket and stapler. And it's useful to at least make clear the intention to include supplies by adding to your list a phrase such as: "All office and cleaning supplies ordinarily kept on premises."

Leasehold improvements also belong on the list. The legal owner of items such as refrigeration, ovens and fire security system (in the case of a restaurant), counters, shelves and lighting (in a retail store), and trade fixtures used in other businesses, should be spelled out in the lease. You want to determine if equipment and fixtures attached to the walls and ceiling, and affixed to the floor, belong to the real estate – meaning they are owned by the landlord – or to the lessee who operates the business. In either event, your agreement should specify exactly which items are to be included in the sale.

Inventory

Whether the inventory of merchandise held for resale is included in the price of the business, or is to be purchased separately by the buyer at close of escrow, should be made clear in the purchase contract. If not, a misunderstanding is almost certainly going to occur. The buyer will voice the expectation that the linens, pillows and quilts sold in the bedding store are part of what she is buying, while the seller invariably believes that the sales price is for other assets of the business, and that the wholesale value of the inventory should be calculated in addition to the business' sales price.

Not only do principals have to agree about the treatment of inventory, they also should prepare to determine its exact value – since that can vary from one day to the next – at the time the deal is closed. If inventory will be included in the price, there should be an understanding to adjust the price so it corresponds with the amount by which the inventory in the final count is different from the value anticipated in the sales agreement. If, for example, the agreement specifies that the $150,000 sale price includes $22,500 of inventory at cost, and a final count reveals a total of $24,000 in inventory, the sales price would be adjusted to $151,500. Of course it works the other way: The sales price would be reduced in the event inventory value at close is lower than the amount anticipated in the contract.

Regardless of whether the business' sale price includes inventory, the physical count should be conducted right before the close, with both buyer and seller involved. Once all the items have been counted and a total value calculated after consulting the price lists, the final figure is furnished to the escrow service or escrow attorney.

Closing instructions from the stakeholder, either an escrow company or a business attorney, will have the buyer bring the specified amount in a cashier's check. Or, if parties prefer, any adjustments can be made in the face amount of the promissory note due to the seller.

Agreements with other parties

The premises lease, the Yellow Pages advertising contract and any other agreements to which the business is party should be noted in the purchase agreement and transferred to the buyer at the close of escrow. If there are exceptions to this, because there are agreements to which the new owner does not want to be obligated, those exceptions should be stated.

Does the business have marketing arrangements with other organizations? There may be sponsorship of a local athletic team, a contract with a coupon distributor, a billboard deal or advertising in local periodicals and buying guides. The buyer wants to learn about all of these programs, and determine which agreements the business wants to maintain. And if possible, get confirmation from the third parties that they will continue to do business under the same terms with the new ownership.

Customer contracts ordinarily are included in the sale and should be specifically mentioned and explained in the purchase/sale agreement.

Other assets

In addition to the agreements noted above, there may be licenses, patents, franchise rights and other assets which have value and are important to the successful operation of the business. They should be specifically identified in the offer as well as in any subsequent contracts involved in the purchase of the business. The buyer will do well to verify the assignability of any agreements or rights belonging to the business being purchased. If any of the contracts with third parties are not assignable, the buyer should be aware of that so other arrangements can be made. And if certain contracts are important to the business and cannot be obtained by the buyer, it might be necessary to cancel the transaction.

It's usually a good idea to attach as exhibits to the purchase contract, copies of any agreements with other parties, as well as permits, licenses, patents, exclusive marketing rights and whatever other pacts belong to, or confer rights on the business. Are they to be transferred to the new owner? By having all of these items identified in the agreement between buyer and seller, there is less chance for confusion or misunderstanding about what is included in the business sale.

Seller agreements

The seller's covenant not to compete can be important to the buyer not only because of the protection it affords but also because it is an asset that can be written off in the buyer's tax returns over the life of the agreement. In the case of a three year covenant, for example, the buyer will be able to deduct an amount equal to one third of its value from taxable profits, each year for three years.

And the training agreement, while it usually is not treated as a depreciable asset for tax purposes, can be important as an opportunity for the buyer to get a quick education about the business and to use the seller in the marketing effort. The smart buyer asks the seller to make an introduction to key customers and to provide insight into how to work with them to maximum advantage. These are assets which the buyer should make sure are clearly defined in the agreement. They can be detailed within the text of the basic contract, or can be expressed in separate documents used as addenda to the contract.

Buyer's agreement

The buyer might want to reiterate his or her pledge to maintain the non-disclosure of the seller and the business information, throughout the process of the sale.

Goodwill

Having no significant tax planning value, and representing a less tangible part of the deal than many of the other assets, the goodwill is, nevertheless, an important part of the business you are buying. Among the components considered to be included in goodwill are the company's name and reputation, and the expectation of continuing business from its customer base. (This is understood more clearly by contrast with a brand new company which has not yet established an identity in the marketplace, and is still focusing its efforts on gaining customers. For a newly formed enterprise building goodwill requires months or years of continuous effort.) While it's generally understood that the company's goodwill is included in the sale, I think it's a good idea for the buyer to make sure it is referenced in the contract, as one of the business' assets being purchased.

Also to be mentioned as an asset being purchased is the customer list. This is generally considered to fall within the category of goodwill, although court cases have established the customer list – at least in some industries – to be a separate item. Make sure that you get a list of customers or a file drawer of customer account information when you take over the business. And be certain to include customer list in the purchase agreement as one of the assets that will be transferred to you.

Allocation of purchase price

It would be easy to simply assume that the sum of the values of all the assets sold is equal to the total purchase price, without assigning – or allocating – a specific value to each item.

The tax law, however, makes it mandatory that the agreement include the specific amount of the total purchase price that is allocated to each asset. And the allocation should be agreed on by both parties, even though every asset may have a different value for the buyer than for the seller.

The buyer, for example, considers the training agreement and covenant not to compete to be more valuable than does the seller. And because each has a different depreciation program, one party will consider the depreciable hard assets to be worth more than will the other party.

At issue, of course is the tax treatment for dollars allocated to these assets. What is ordinarily in the best interest of the buyer, from a tax standpoint, usually is contrary to what is preferred in terms of the seller's tax planning strategy.

An allocation is probably included in the seller's offering package. You, the buyer, would be smart to review this information with a tax specialist before deciding whether to accept the allocation as structured by the seller, or to propose a different allocation, more favorable to your tax planning. This matter can become a subject of negotiations between buyer and seller, and should be resolved at the time the other particulars – price and terms of the transaction – are worked out. The allocation belongs with the purchase contract as an addendum, or as a provision in the body of the offer, and the contract.

As an example, a possible allocation for a café selling at $200,000, could be $50,000 for equipment, $25,000 for leasehold improvements, $20,000 for training, $30,000 for a three-year non-compete agreement, and the balance of $75,000 for goodwill. If this is acceptable to the parties, it would be part of their purchase agreement.

Representations and warranties

Your agreement with the seller should contain the seller's assertions that everything told to you about the business is true and accurate and that there are no material facts being withheld from you. This provision in a contract frequently is ignored or overlooked because it seems like so much "legalese."

But it's good to include this provision in your agreement because it is meant to protect you. In many cases of fraud and deception by a seller, it was a paragraph about representations and warranties which was cited by a buyer in pursuit of his or her legal rights.

What Usually is Not Sold

By definition, the asset purchase that you hope to be engaged in when you've found the right business will call for you to buy the items reviewed earlier in this chapter. And you'll want to receive those assets free and clear of any liabilities, liens or encumbrances. This should be clearly specified in your agreement with the seller.

This applies also to any legal claims that might arise after you take over the business but are based in circumstances that existed before the company was yours. An illustration is the experience of a new owner in a dry cleaning business who was confronted by an unhappy customer, complaining about a sweater, worth $150, ruined by the company the week before the buyer and seller closed escrow.

The buyer insisted the problem was not his fault because the business did not belong to him when the damage occurred. The customer, predictably, stated that he didn't care who owned the business when the garment was damaged, as far as he was concerned, it was the company's fault, and he wanted the company to replace the sweater or give him $150.

The buyer wisely delegated the problem to the seller, letting him know it was his responsibility, because their agreement said the buyer would get the business free and clear of any obligations, and the seller would protect the buyer in any action of this kind.

And you want to make sure the seller has paid or agrees to take care of all of the payables that are due from the business. Some of the creditors – people or companies owed money by the business – may be regular suppliers. So it's important their bills are paid and that they intend to continue the relationship with your new business. It's not fair to you, if they want to cut off supplies to you because the old owner was behind in making payments.

If you do agree to assume any of the seller's obligations, you should receive a compensating benefit from the seller. In other words, if a seller owes a vendor $10,000, the buyer may want to assume that obligation in return for a $10,000 reduction in the purchase price.

It's probably best, incidentally, for the seller to keep the receivables since he or she is responsible for the payables. The money owed to the business before you take over rightfully belongs to the seller. There's no reason, however, why you can't arrange to collect from customers on their old accounts – and turn those receipts over to the seller – as you interact with these customers regarding new business. Just make sure they understand the payments on old business go to the seller, and they have a responsibility to remain current with you on new business.

Another way for the new owner to manage old receivables is to actually buy them at a discount from the seller, then keep the proceeds as they are collected. As an example, if the seller is carrying $5,000 in receivables, the buyer could pay $4,000 (a customary 80%) to the seller for the right to those funds. Then as the receivables are collected, they belong to the buyer.

Conclusion

Whether contained in a Letter of Intent (LOI) or a standard offer form, the statement of your terms for purchasing a small business should be presented to the seller along with details of your work experience and financial ability. The offer includes identity of the parties and the business, description of the deal structure, reference to exhibits or addenda that detail the assets included, seller's and buyer's agreements, contingencies and a recognition of what actions need to be taken, including the opening of a business escrow, in order to complete the transaction. Time requirements also are included for those responsibilities still to be completed.

The various assets that should be transferred to the buyer include tangible and intangible items and should be specified in the purchase contract. Not included should be the seller's various long-term and short-term liabilities and any encumbrances against the business.

KEY POINTS FROM THIS CHAPTER

❖ *Most offers to purchase a small business are made on one of the standard offer forms which then constitute the contract between buyer and seller, once parties are in agreement on the terms of the deal. A sample offer form is available at www.USABizMart.com Select the "Tools" tab, then go to the "Forms" section, in which you will find the Conditional Purchase and Sale of Assets Agreement.*

❖ *The Letter of Intent (LOI) is used for larger and more complex transaction which will be conducted according to a purchase agreement prepared by an attorney. The LOI states the buyer's intent and spells out the terms so parties can determine if they are in agreement before they proceed to have the contract prepared.*

❖ *The buyer is advised to submit a history of work experience and details of his or her financial ability along with the offer or LOI. This can help to persuade the seller about the seriousness and capabilities of the buyer.*

❖ *Once presented with an offer or LOI, the seller can accept all of the terms, or reject it because of differences over some of the terms, or accept the offer subject to a counter offer, which means the seller wants to specify some alternative terms.*

❖ *The buyer also can respond with a counter offer to a counter offer from the seller. If parties want to have a transaction and yet are unable to agree on all aspects, as demonstrated by the exchange of counteroffers, the best idea might be for them to meet across the bargaining table and attempt to go over every item, one my one, until they have a complete agreement, or until they discover they are unable to come to agreement, which means they should not waste more time.*

❖ *The offer should include the identity of the parties and the business, the particulars of the proposed deal structure, and a description of what tasks and obligations need to be accomplished, and when, before the business can change hands.*

❖ *Because two reasonable and honest people still can have different interpretations about the meaning of an unclear provision, it is important that the offer and the purchase agreement describe, as explicitly as possible, what you expect to receive in your purchase of the business.*

❖ Among the assets that should be specifically mentioned by the buyer as included with the sale is the business name and its trade style, or logo.

❖ A list of all capital assets to be sold should be included in the offer, and then in the contract. It's best if the list is as complete as parties can make it. Leasehold improvements, though a different class of assets than tools and equipment, also should be included.

❖ Whether or not the value of the inventory is to be included in the purchase price must be stated in the offer. Include an approximate inventory value and note that it is subject to change, once the actual count of inventory is conducted immediately prior to completing the transaction.

❖ The premises lease, advertising contracts, deals with customers and any other legal agreements relied on in conduct of the business should be listed as being transferred from seller to buyer. It's useful for a copy of each of these documents to be included with the offer, and then attached once the offer becomes the purchase contract.

❖ Among the seller agreements that become part of the finished contract are the pledge to train the buyer in the business and the non-compete covenant, which will extend for a period of months or years beyond close of the transaction, as agreed on by the buyer and seller.

❖ The chief buyer agreement in a transaction – beyond dealing in good faith – is to honor the non-disclosure/confidentiality agreement until the end of the transaction.

❖ Hard to measure or value, the goodwill of a company being purchased is probably the most important asset the buyer will acquire. In most situations, the goodwill includes the customer list, although there are industries in which it is treated as a separate asset.

❖ Buyer and seller are required by the Internal Revenue Service (IRS) to include an allocation of the purchase price in the purchase agreement. The allocation includes a specific value for each asset, and those values will be reflected in the tax returns of the parties to the transaction. For example, the value for depreciable assets will be shown in the buyer's return because of the depreciation that will be claimed. In the seller's return, the value of these assets will be compared to the value shown in prior returns so a determination can be made whether the seller gained or lost money by the sale of these assets, and whether or not a capital gains tax is due.

❖ *The seller's representations and warranties refer to the viability of the business and the truth and accuracy of any statements about it that were made by the seller. The buyer's representations have to do with his or her ability to perform according to the contract.*

❖ *The purchase agreement states what the buyer expects to purchase. Also mentioned is that all assets are free and clear of liens or encumbrances. The buyer may choose to accept the business subject to (that is, along with) the claims against its assets, and/or take on some of the debt. In that event, the purchase price would be adjusted appropriately.*

❖ *The seller ordinarily pays off all payables owed to vendors by the business and collects the receivables due to the business. Variations on this arrangement are possible if parties arrange for the buyer to collect receivables and/or pay payables.*

CHAPTER TWELVE

SOME NEGOTIATING TIPS

Children are admonished by their parents, after a trip to the circus, not to try and mimic the dangerous stunts they saw performed by professionals.

I won't give you the same advice about representing yourself when negotiating to purchase a small business – for one thing, you can't break any bones by failing to execute a move properly, while discussing a deal. But if you're inexperienced at reaching an agreement while balancing between what you need, and what the other party is trying to achieve, it could be hazardous to your financial health to do this yourself.

If you have a competent broker or agent working with you, it's best to leave the negotiating up to him or to her. And your job is to let the representative know what you want and what you won't accept.

Even with professional help, it doesn't hurt for you – whether you're the buyer or the seller – to gain some insight into what can constitute intelligent negotiating. You might find you have a gift for it and your input will be helpful in establishing a workable package of price and terms.

Here are some of the ideas which help guide skilled negotiators.

Don't Take it Personally

You should know, for instance, that there's little room for emotions when talking about your money. For some people, of course, the fear of loss or the anticipation of gain can evoke strong feelings, and these get revealed in a display of one kind or another. But it's best if you can control the outward signs of your anger, elation, sadness, frustration or whatever you are feeling when your proposals are rejected, or even when your suggestions are adopted, as you conduct discussions with the other party in the transaction for a small business.

The necessity of separating emotions from business should seem obvious. And yet I have seen intelligent, successful business people who react as if they or their ideas are being criticized severely, when a seller explains the reasons for not wanting to accept an offer, or a buyer discusses the rational behind not meeting the seller's price.

Can you separate your business dealings from the emotional investment you've made in your campaign to buy or to sell a company? Your outbursts may aggravate, scare, intimidate or even please the people sitting on the other side of the table. But it's unlikely the other will change his or her mind about something because of your behavior. And if you are able to keep your feelings in check, you'll come across as a more powerful figure – someone to be reckoned with – and that can help you get some of the concessions you want.

Besides, you'll be able to manage your side of the negotiations from strength, rather than feel vulnerable, victimized and a little scared.

Remain Focused on Your Objective

When you're in the middle of a battle about a particular subject, don't lose sight of what you're trying to accomplish. With a clear objective that you keep in your head – a vision of a completed deal to work for – you're less likely to find yourself heavily engaged in a battle over matters that are much less consequential than your goal. Don't allow yourself to be distracted. And don't fix on a particular issue that's relatively unimportant to you, compared to the accomplishment of the overall objective.

That means, for example that you'll recognize the value of a "bird in hand."

Indeed, the other party may be quite difficult to deal with. And you may feel yourself being pushed toward your limits of patience as well as to the edge of your willingness to negotiate. But are you sure you'd be better off starting from scratch?

If you're the buyer, what if it takes awhile to find another suitable business? What if the next seller isn't any easier to work with than this one?

If you're the seller, what will you have to do in order to get another qualified and motivated customer? Can you work with the one in front of you?

And consider this: Whether you're the buyer or seller, you've devoted a great deal of time and money, taken on the hard work, endured the difficult circumstances and maintained patience during the long process, so that you could achieve your goal. Let that be your mantra when buyer and seller encounter issues that threaten to derail negotiations for the company on which you want to strike a deal. Don't stick stubbornly to a minor issue without being mindful of its overall impact on the deal.

Importance of Flexibility

Certainly, there are matters about which you need to be firm. Some parts of the seller's offering are critical to his or her overall planning, just as some provisions are of prime importance to the buyer. And it might not make sense to enter into a transaction if your most important needs are neglected. But be selective about what requests are true deal killers and which are not.

Is it possible you can seriously consider the other person's desire for a payoff program that's different from what you'd anticipated? Or a different interest rate than you'd planned? These need not ruin your chances for an acceptable contract if there's a way you can accommodate each others' needs. Make an effort to keep the transaction on track without seriously damaging the achievement of your overall objectives.

I've heard a number of stories over the years from business brokers and agents about how their clients became stubborn, rather unnecessarily, over relatively minor matters, and then realized, later on, that they might have had a good deal, had they been a bit more open to other ideas. These are disappointed buyers and sellers who learned, the hard way, that flexibility is an important attribute when you're negotiating over the sale of a small business.

Starting from the Bottom Line

If you know the absolute highest price you'll agree to pay, as well as the point at which the terms of purchase would be unacceptable, you're prepared to enter into negotiations. Assuming that you and a seller are far apart regarding some of the provisions of the contract for your purchase of a business, you can let the other party know that you feel it's worth exploring how a compromise can be reached. It means each of you must be willing to give a little. If you get agreement on this point, it means the other person is willing to try and work out a deal, and will renegotiate where possible.

From that point it's just a matter of discussing each of the issues, perhaps moving back and forth among them – you get a provision important to you, the other party gets his or her terms on another aspect – until either a final agreement is achieved, or it becomes clear that there can't be a deal without going beyond the bottom line that one or both of you has established.

For example, if you are a buyer who is unwilling, under any circumstances, to pay more than $200,000 for the business, and the seller insists that the least she'll accept is $230,000, it's not worth your time to continue discussing the matter. But if the seller says "I'd only agree to $200,000 if I had excellent terms," that might be an opening to continue negotiating.

Suppose the buyer goes along with the seller's strict payoff schedule on the portion of the purchase price being carried back, and also agrees to pay a higher interest rate than originally planned. This is the time to for the buyer to remind the seller that he or she has given in on the last couple of items, and now the seller ought to agree to the buyer's request for an extended period of training. This will allow the purchaser to conserve some of the working capital that would have been used for extra payroll, and will increase the probability that the buyer will be successful in the business.

The value of this style of negotiating is that it recognizes each party has a bottom line that can't be violated, though you don't reveal your positions. You agree to respect each others' thresholds, to end negotiations if a deal can't be struck within the parameters acceptable to both.

But every thing else is fair game, as you work to find some combination of give and take that can lead you to an agreement.

Building from Consensus

Another approach is to explore the issues with the other party about which you can agree. If you see eye-to-eye about some of the terms of the deal, you can then move to those few points on which you do not agree. Then you can chip away at those bones of contention, either by meeting somewhere in the middle, or by taking turns granting a concession. Or both.

I've watched skilled negotiators use this technique very effectively. Sometimes when parties to a transaction in progress reach an impasse, someone will say:

"Let's review again the items that we DO agree on." The object of this exercise, of course, is to concentrate on the positive aspects of your agreement – the areas where you are in concurrence – as a motivation to find a solution for the negotiating points not yet resolved.

Take a Time Out

Experienced negotiators also know the value of postponing further discussion if opposing parties are getting nowhere in their talks. Rather than arriving at the conclusion that there is no way a deal can be struck, why not reconvene in an hour, or in a few days, when tempers have cooled and principals have had a chance to think through their needs and objectives? A buyer and seller may be able to come back after rethinking their positions and work out a satisfactory deal with provisions they couldn't see clearly in the heat of negotiations, before the break.

Of course, the choice to separate temporarily, for a cooling off period, can work to the detriment of an agreement. It's possible, during the time between negotiating sessions, that one or both of the participants will decide they are not willing to continue negotiating with the other person along the same lines

In either event, the choice to "cool it" for awhile, usually gives people the opportunity to gain some perspective on the issues at hand, so each can determine what is in his or her best interests.

If you and the other party find yourselves spinning your negotiating wheels and not making progress, perhaps a time out is the best choice.

Conclusion

It's easy to get distracted in the middle of negotiations for the purchase of a small business, and to believe that the other party is trying to take advantage of you. But if you try on some of the ideas proposed here, you may be able to see the situation in less threatening terms. And that may help you to continue to engage in negotiations until you arrive at a deal that accommodates the transfer of the business along the lines of––if not blissful ecstasy – at least, terms you can live with.

KEY POINTS FROM THIS CHAPTER

❖ *Considering that you, the buyer of a small business, and most any seller have contradictory objectives, it can be very difficult to negotiate an agreement. And this challenge is compounded in situations in which buyers are their own representatives, not able to benefit from the services of an objective intermediary who can sometimes work out these differences between parties.*

❖ *It's useful to try and keep your emotions in check when talking business. It is understandable that people have strong feelings when their fortunes are at stake in their discussions, but showing anger, frustration, even elation, makes it harder to maintain the "cool head" needed to arrive at intelligent decisions in difficult negotiations. A seller's desire to receive more money than the buyer wants to pay for a business need not be interpreted as a criticism about either individual, or that individual's business style.*

❖ *Remembering the overall objective – to reach agreement at workable terms – can help to prevent obsessing about details of a transaction that, in the long run, are not critically important.*

❖ *However, buyers and sellers are not urged to agree to provisions that are contrary to their best interests. To decide what is and is not in your best interests, requires that you take a look at the transaction as a whole and consider long and short-term costs as well as gains.*

❖ *One way to bring parties together on an agreement is for each to determine their bottom line for every issue – the full extent to which they will agree regarding price, terms, and the other components of a purchase/sales contract. Then try to compromise on terms in a way that these bottom lines aren't crossed.*

❖ *Another negotiating strategy to achieve a deal is to start with discussion of every item about which parties are in accord. Then build on this success by trying to reach a fair consensus on the other issues, one by one. Sometimes if there are two problem areas, the resolution is for one party to win on one, the other party gets the second.*

❖ *A timeout is an excellent way for people to clear their heads from the intense, stressful experience of negotiating a business deal. Once they've had a chance to gain a broader perspective it may be easier to reach agreement or, alternatively, to see that there is no likelihood of agreement.*

CHAPTER THIRTEEN

THE DEAL

In the preceding chapters, I've endeavored to offer sellers and buyers of small businesses some insights into the tasks of preparing your company or preparing yourself to go to market, to do the work needed to be successful and to negotiate a deal that represents a win-win for you and the other party. The culmination of all your efforts to date is represented by the purchase and sales agreement. This document, which is likely to be the same form used for the offer, articulates the provisions by which you and the person on the other side of the bargaining table are prepared to complete your transaction – the blueprint for your business arrangement. And it is the definitive record – if needed in the future – of the deal by which the business changes hands, putting the buyer in the position of owner, and freeing the seller to get on with other things in life.

The topics to be discussed as components of the deal already were touched on when the focus was on the making of an offer to purchase a business. It might be useful now to go into a few of these matters in a bit more detail so that you know what items should comprise your deal. Remember that you can get a widely used contract blank at no charge by downloading the template from *www.USABizMart.com* Go to the "Tools" tab, open the "Forms" folder to find the agreement.

What's Included in the Purchase/Sales Contract

About 90% of the purchases of small businesses involve business assets, rather than corporate stock, and this discussion is confined to the more common type of transaction.

Starting with the basics, a purchase/sales agreement on the company you are buying or selling will first note the date and identify the purchaser, include name and address of the subject business, then will state the purchase price and detail how it is to be paid. The amount of down payment is noted, then terms of payoff are spelled out, with an exact description of the note structure. For example, if the seller is carrying back a portion of the purchase price, does the note call for regular monthly payments over a specified time, one or more balloon payments, a delay of payments, or months when payments may be skipped? This is explained in detail in the purchase/sale agreement so the instructions are clear for the escrow service or escrow attorney, who will be charged with the responsibility of drafting the note, or notes, when it's time to complete your transaction.

The escrow service or stakeholder also will need specific instructions about collateralizing any notes. Will the business assets provide the security? Have you and the other party agreed on other collateral to be used, such as buyer's personal or real property, to back up the obligation? Details about this part of the agreement need to be included in the purchase/sales agreement, in the discussion about the promissory notes.

If additional financing is required to complete the purchase, that fact should be addressed in detail in the contact. The agreement can even specify the finance terms that are acceptable to the buyer, with respect to length of payoff and interest rate charged, so there is no question as to what will be required to remove this contingency.

The lease and capital assets

Determination of the leasehold interest belonging to the business is frequently treated in the early paragraphs of the agreement. Will the lease be transferred as is? Is there a contingency regarding the buyer being able to obtain the lease at the same terms? Is a new lease required as part of the deal?

What follows in the agreement is the detail of items included in the sale. As this text is concerned with the asset sale, I recommend that the individual items be specifically noted, usually on a separate list. Such list should cover all capital equipment, including vehicles, if there are trucks or cars belonging to the business and part of the sale.

And typically the leasehold improvements are included as assets. They may be given a value in the transaction and are used by the owner of the business. Yet these items ultimately might be written off the business books if they are attached to the real estate and belong to the landlord. Leases ordinarily stipulate whether title to leasehold improvements stays with the owner of the real property or with the tenant who owns the business.

Inventory

Treatment of inventory – how much is anticipated at cost, at close of escrow, and whether it is to be included as part of the purchase price – is a subject that needs to be addressed in the buy/sell document. If the purchase price includes the inventory of parts, supplies and materials, the actual sale price will be adjusted at the closing, by the variation in value of inventory – when it is counted and computed – from the projected amount.

With brokers involved in a transaction, and a commission based on total price, the principals usually are encouraged by their broker representatives to include inventory as part of the deal. Inventory inclusion boosts the business sales price, and hence the commission. A seller, however, should handle the inventory in whatever way he or she deems easier and more appropriate to the circumstances.

Employment agreements

It is likely that as part of the deal, the seller has agreed with the buyer to be employed with the company for a period of time following the close. In most cases, this does not mean the seller is added to the payroll, but has taken on the assignment of introducing the buyer to customers, suppliers and other individuals important to the functioning of the company. And the seller will train the buyer in the operation of the business. The terms of this understanding should be noted, as they will be incorporated into a training agreement, usually prepared in escrow and presented to the seller and the buyer at the close. Depending on what you've worked out, the training contract may require the seller to spend some time at the place of business, or to be available by phone for consultation, or both. Usually, the training period is defined in terms of the number of days or weeks that it extends beyond the close.

The other common form of employment contract is the covenant not to compete, in which the seller agrees that he or she won't be active as a principal, employee or contractor for any firm engaged in the same business as the one being sold. This agreement also has a specified period after which it expires, usually coinciding with the length of time provided for paying off the note, say, three or five years. Thus, when the buyer is finished paying the seller on the obligation, the seller is no longer required to refrain from competing with the seller's former business. There should be a geographic definition for the covenant, setting the number of miles from the subject business in which the seller is not allowed to compete or work for a competitor. The buyer of your tree trimming service, for example, would not want you to conduct that activity within the area – usually a few square miles – where current customers are located. That is understandable. But there is no reason you should not be permitted to open such a business, even the following week, if you were to move to another part of the state. The time and distance requirements on the covenant need to be included in the contract between buyer and seller. These terms then will be incorporated into the covenant not to compete which, like the training agreement, will be presented to the parties for approval when the deal is closed.

Special provisions

Are there any additional agreements made part of your purchase/sales contract to deal with special problems? Suppose, for example, the buyer worries about the loss of business if a major customer – rumored to be moving from the area – does relocate soon after close, and the company (when it belongs to the buyer) loses the customer's business. If the seller agreed to compensate the buyer for part of this loss, those details should be spelled out in the buy/sell agreement and may become part of the note and closing instructions.

Items excluded

In many cases, there are items which are present in the place of business that are not included in the deal. It may be sufficient for parties to the agreement to concur on a standard provision in your contract which states that anything not on the list of assets transferred is deemed to be excluded from the sale.

But it doesn't hurt to create a separate list of excluded items when preparing the agreement, so there is no confusion or misunderstanding about what is and is not to go to the buyer at the close.

Some years ago, the buyer of a children's clothing store became upset when he took possession of his business and realized that a number of antique dolls that were prominently displayed when he viewed the business, were no longer at the premises. After a few angry phone conversations, he learned that the seller had taken these items and had not considered them to be part of the deal. An argument followed in which the parties threatened to sue one another over this matter.

The dispute was kept out of court with a final settlement in which some cash went back to the buyer. The parties recognized, after the aggravation they experienced and the payments made to their lawyers to work out a compromise, that they should have compiled a list of items excluded from sale at the beginning of their negotiations.

As noted earlier, many cash items on the balance sheet – particularly receivables and payables – of the business are ordinarily considered to be excluded from the deal. There can be an arrangement, of course, by which the buyer keeps some of the seller's assets and liabilities if such provisions are requested by the parties and the purchase price is properly adjusted to reflect their agreement.

Contingencies

After specifying those assets being sold and for how much, and noting specifically what is excluded, the contract deals with the procedures needed for the transaction to be completed.

Just as the buyer and seller in the transaction for a home use contingencies to protect themselves from having to perform till all the required actions are completed and the facts are in, you and the other party are waiting for certain things to take place before you move forward on your business deal. It is the contingencies part of your agreement which outlines the work you both have to do and describes what has to be satisfactorily resolved in order for the transaction to proceed to the next step. We already have touched on a number of these contingencies. They cover the transfer, renewal or rewriting of the lease, the buyer's satisfactory review of the business books and records, the buyer's ability to obtain a certain amount of financing and also the satisfactory inspection and review, by the buyer, of any other issues that pertain to the viability of the business. Whatever they are, all contingencies need to be clearly stated in your agreement so that both buyer and seller know exactly what needs to take place to have a deal.

Unlike other components of the transaction, the contingencies are not usually included in the escrow papers, for the reason that these items should have been resolved prior to getting into escrow, and are no longer at issue at that point.

As was pointed out in a previous chapter, the buyer's time limit to review the business records and remove this contingency should be brief enough to keep things moving forward at a steady pace. While seven to ten business days is a usual time frame for the buyer's conduct of due diligence, there may be delays, waiting for the landlord's participation so the buyer can verify that the lease will be satisfactorily transferred or that a new and acceptable lease will be granted. And if the deal is dependent on a lender because of a financing contingency, there also may be a delay past your seven to ten day deadline while the money source crosses the "T"s, dots the "I"s, and determines if and when the cash will be forthcoming.

Here's the seller's chance to be the hero and keep moving your deal through this step. If you followed the advice offered in an earlier chapter (about preparing your business for sale) you may already have "shopped" the company's borrowing needs and all you have to do is produce a qualified buyer to get the loan started. I also advocate that buyers work on getting pre-approved while searching for a business to buy. This way, buyers can quickly get the money needed, and can demonstrate to skeptical sellers that they're ready and able to do business.

Despite the best planning, of course, there may be delays that are out of your control. That's when it's a good idea to make certain you and the other party remain in contract. You each can sign a separate note or jointly approve an addendum that refers to the contract and stipulates that you're both in accord about the likely delay and about a new deadline for contingency removal.

And what about seller's contingency removal? The seller may need some time – seven to ten days while the buyer is conducting due diligence – to verify the buyer's creditworthiness and be satisfied that this is a suitable candidate for new owner of the business as well as someone to whom the seller is willing to loan money.

Escrow

Somewhere in the agreement parties should include the name and address of the escrow lawyer or company and set out a plan for the buyer to deliver, to escrow, his or her deposit check – the one that was presented with the offer. It's customary for the buyer to increase the deposit when opening escrow and this provision should be included in your agreement. Also, determine who will pay for escrow services. They start at about $1,000 and go up from there, depending on the size of the transaction and how much work is to be done preparing various documents and making sure to comply with legal requirements in completing the transaction. Local business brokers can make recommendations as to competent escrow services or you can find some suggestions by selecting the "Resources" tab at *www.USABizMart.com* While the question of who pays this cost is sometimes determined with further negotiations between buyer and seller, the parties usually make the choice to split the escrow expenses, and this is recommended as the easiest way to resolve the matter. If you're in the mood to do a little more wheeling and dealing, you can use this point as a bargaining chip. If, during negotiations, the other party is resisting an idea that's important to you, perhaps you can prevail by offering to pay all escrow fees if the other party will go along with you on that point. Alternatively, when it comes time to insert into your agreement who will pay for the escrow service, you may want to remind the other person of your last concession during the negotiations, and then announce: "You owe me one," suggesting that the other party pick up the escrow's bill.

The date for closing the deal should be specified in your contract. Don't forget the ticking of the clock that will occur while the work is being done to remove contingencies. You want to remove all contingencies before the final process is started and before you've incurred any closing fees. And then there is frequently a waiting period during which the creditors are notified of the intended deal, and they have a window – in most states it's around two or three weeks – to submit any claims they might have against the business being sold. Keeping these time-consuming projects in mind, you can refer to your calendar and decide when you and the other party can schedule the transfer to take place.

Whether you are the buyer or seller, pay attention to how much time might be required and make sure that corresponds with your timing. More than one seller who failed to allow enough closing time was surprised and disappointed to learn that a deal would drag over into the following fiscal or calendar year, rendering a seller's clever tax planning totally unusable.

Non-disclosure reminder

Because the buyer's careful handling of the seller's confidential information is so important, I recommend repeating the idea that these secrets are to remain secrets throughout the process in which the buyer is investigating the business. It might be worth adding a paragraph at the end of the agreement that reiterates the importance of non-disclosure. In signing the contract for the purchase of the business, the buyer should be reminded about this principle.

Due Diligence

With a signed agreement under your belts, you and the other party move from the arms-length attitude marking negotiations, to a new level of intimacy in your business dealings. From this point on, it is hoped you'll be working together.

You're hard effort is not over, of course--either for the buyer or seller. I'll take up the matter of due diligence in more detail in a later chapter.

Standard provisions

The representations and warranties of the parties, the remedies in the event of a legal dispute – arbitration or lawsuit with prevailing party receiving attorney fees – and the other standard legal provisions which are present in most business contracts also belong in the purchase/sales agreement on a small business. Each principal in a transaction of this kind is well advised to include a contingency that calls for the approval of the contract by his or her attorney, before moving forward.

For Franchises

If you are involved as buyer or seller of a franchised business, you may receive a contract form from the franchisor. Additionally, your franchisor may be able to act as the escrow service (or may insist on it). Determine which of you will pay the franchise transfer fees, if any. Some franchise owners don't get assistance from the franchisor when it comes to selling. If that includes your deal, it might be a good idea to include franchisor approval of the transfer as a contingency.

Conclusion

The purchase/sales contract that parties hammer out after engaging in negotiations provides the blue print for the plan by which seller will go on to something else, and buyer will take over the business. The agreement reviews the details – the price, terms, and allocation – for your transaction. And it lists precisely what is and what is not included in the transaction. The contingencies are noted along with the time in which they are to be removed. An escrow company or attorney should be named and you and the other party will be prepared to take the buyer's check to open an escrow as soon as the due diligence process is completed.

And that, the critical due diligence, needs your utmost attention if you are the seller of the business. No one else understands and can sell the business, and can reassure a hesitant buyer, the way you can.

KEY POINTS FROM THIS CHAPTER

❖ *Having reached agreement on the sale of a small business, parties can now begin the work involved in completing their deal, adhering to the provisions of the purchase/sales agreement (often expanding on the document in which the offer was made,) and engaging in the due diligence process.*

❖ *Some 90% of small business sales involve the transfer of business assets, as distinct from corporate stock sales. This review focuses on the more common type of transaction.*

❖ *A sample purchase/sale agreement can be viewed and downloaded by visiting www.USABizMart.com Click on the "Tools" tab and go to the "Forms" folder for this blank document.*

❖ *Seller financing should be explained in detail so that parties are clear about what was agreed, and so that escrow has explicit instructions for preparation of needed documents, such as any promissory notes.*

❖ *A clear statement of what is included in the sale – a complete list of capital assets is recommended – should be part of the principals' contract. Following is the agreement as to inventory – will a certain amount (at cost) be included in the sale price or considered an addition to the price?*

❖ *Employment contracts in the purchase/sales agreement usually refer to the seller's obligation to train the buyer – with specifics about where and for how long that will take place – and to not compete with the buyer's new business for a specified period of time in a defined geographic area. The covenant not to compete is often timed to expire when the buyer's obligation to the seller – if the seller is financing part of the purchase price – is paid in full.*

❖ *Any special arrangements or understandings agreed on by parties should be explained in detail so there is no confusion about this part of the deal, and so that the escrow office is equipped to prepare any supporting documents necessitated by such agreements.*

❖ *Those items not to be included in the business sale might be listed and approved by buyer and seller so there is no misunderstanding on this point.*

❖ *Any contingencies agreed on by the parties, that need to be satisfied and removed prior to opening escrow, should be specified in the purchase/sales contract. Contingencies probably include buyer obtaining the premises lease and being satisfied with a review of the business books, records and other information. And the seller may make the deal contingent on being satisfied after review of the buyer's financial standing and credit worthiness.*

❖ *The agreement then reviews the matter of escrow: Who will manage the completion of the agreement and compliance with the law, and who will pay for these services? A 50/50 split of costs between buyer and seller is a common practice.*

❖ *An anticipated closing date is noted, after parties compute the time that will be needed in order to comply with any legal requirements for the sale of business assets.*

❖ *The agreement also should include representations and warranties from both buyer and seller to provide protection for each other. The buyer acknowledges that he or she will conduct due diligence and rely on those findings to decide whether to go forward with the purchase. The seller warrants that equipment is in good, working order, the inventory is merchantable, and that there are no known factors, undisclosed to the buyer, which might affect the fortunes of the business. Buyers often agree that if they fail to complete the transaction after removal of contingencies, their seller will be allowed to collect the buyer's money on deposit as liquidated damages.*

❖ *Sellers do well to remain closely involved in the buyer's due diligence work. A number of sales have gone off track at this point and may have been saved had the seller intervened when the buyer ran into questions or problems.*

❖ *There may be delays in the process as buyer and seller are relying on others – lenders and landlord, for example – to be involved in the work of removing contingencies. It is useful for the principles in the transaction to agree in writing to any extensions of the deadlines, necessitated by these delays, in order to remain "in contract."*

❖ *Franchise business owners may find the franchisor has provided all the resources needed to establish a deal and conduct escrow. If not, your contract with the other party should be contingent on franchisor approval of the sale.*

CHAPTER FOURTEEN

PURCHASE PRICE ALLOCATION

Now's the time for a reality check. And it's a reminder about the importance of planning ahead when selling your company or planning your purchase of a small business. This reminder was first suggested, some pages back, when the discussion focused on the recommended preparations before a business goes on the market. The point was made that it's best to work out an allocation of purchase price beforehand.

The purpose in treating tax consequences in more detail in this chapter is not to give you great tax advice so that you're prepared to beat the system. It's the job of your tax attorney or accountant to recommend the best way to structure a business sales deal based on a number of factors, including your overall financial circumstances, the type of planning in which you've engaged previously, and the relative values of the assets you're selling or purchasing.

My purpose is to urge that you seek out that advice and to let you know how important it might be, particularly for sellers. Your tax planning determines how much money you get to keep, net of taxes, from the proceeds in the sale of your business. And for buyers, it's important to set up your books so that you can maintain some tax benefits in the years to come. These next few pages will offer an overview of the taxability of your assets, and familiarize you with a few general rules so that you can begin the tax plan part of your sale.

But remember that it is your tax advisor who can verify that you're doing the most intelligent things to reduce your tax exposure as a consequence of your transaction. And ask for help fine tuning your plan so you can enjoy maximum benefit from your strategy.

Allocating the Purchase Price

U. S. Tax Law regards the sale of your business as a taxable event and holds you responsible for determining a specific value for each asset sold, enabling the IRS to calculate the amount of any taxes due. The purchase price allocation is the mechanism with which a seller declares the amount of the total price assigned to every item in the deal. So, for example, when you present your offering to the marketplace, you may declare that the $250,000 asking price includes $80,000 of capital equipment, $100,000 in goodwill, $15,000 for leasehold improvements, $30,000 for inventory (at cost), and the balance of $25,000 divided equally between the training you'll provide for the buyer and the covenant not to compete.

Where exactly do these numbers come from?

The amount allocated to inventory is likely to be the closest to actual cost of all your assets. If a physical inventory at close of escrow reveals that in fact, you have $30,000 invested at cost in this asset, there is no taxable event. You enjoyed no gain; suffered no loss.

That leaves the remainder of assets possibly subject to taxation. And because each item will fall into either one or the other of two broad categories of taxable assets, your allocation should be designed to distribute them in a way that minimizes tax exposure.

The two tax categories, as you probably know, are ordinary income – assessed at your tax rate based on earnings, and capital gains tax – prescribed by laws covering capital assets. As ordinary income is usually taxed at a higher rate than capital gains, you probably want to allocate as much of the proceeds from your sale into the capital gains category. That's the guideline followed in the allocation noted above.

Ordinary Income Items

The revenue received as a consequence of most every employment agreement is considered to be ordinary income, taxable at the higher rate. The seller's promise to train a buyer for three months following close of escrow is an employment contract, even though no one was added to the payroll. Also considered an employment agreement is the covenant not to compete. In this case you, the seller, are agreeing not to work, and the payment you receive under this contract is regarded simply as ordinary income, similar to wages, commissions or consulting fees.

Any wonder why, in the example above, the total portion of the purchase price allocated to the items subject to ordinary gain is only 10% of the total? And everything else on the list of assets is considered a capital asset, subject to a lighter tax hit, and so is granted a much higher figure in the allocation.

The simple plan here, of course, is to report the lowest possible value for assets taxed at the higher rate, and a higher value for those items subject to less taxation. But there's an added challenge for all parties involved in the sale of a business: Any allocation favoring the seller's situation is probably detrimental to the buyer's tax plan. And visa versa.

This means that even when an agreement about price, terms, length of training and covenant is achieved, the buyer and seller may have to return to the negotiating table to work out an allocation about which both sides can agree. And I do recommend that you each report the same allocation. Some buyers and sellers feel they should be entitled to apply their individual valuations to the assets that change hands. In other words, they agree to not agree on this matter.

It's a risky tactic however, because if the IRS happens to choose their transaction as one of the deals it picks out at random for a compliance review, it likely will disallow both allocations, on the basis that they don't agree. This agency of the Federal government reasons that if a seller received a certain sum for an asset, such as a company's goodwill, that figure should be the exact amount paid by the buyer. Finding a discrepancy, the IRS will probably rewrite the allocations in a way that requires parties to pay the maximum amount of tax possible.

Capital Gains

Calculations of tax exposure for capital assets is more complicated, compared to ordinary income, because it's necessary, first, to determine the book values of the assets, and then to compare those sums to the values declared in the allocation. Any gain (where allocated value exceeds book value) may subject the seller to a capital gains tax, and a decline may mean a loss that can be used to balance out gains taken elsewhere.

As you may be aware, the book value of each asset is arrived at by various computations over the period that a business uses it. Every time an asset, such as a piece of equipment, is acquired, the amount paid for it is entered in the appropriate category on the plus side of the balance sheet. Then, depreciation charges logged into the operating statement each year represent the amount to be deducted from that total asset figure for the period. In many businesses with active programs of acquiring and selling assets, there are a number of additions and subtractions applied to the assets column every year. This is applicable to equipment and leasehold improvements and some "soft" assets like patents, licensing contracts and, in some industries, customer lists.

The connection between book and market value in the case of many business assets does not last long, because once entered onto the books, the numbers representing asset value are subject only to accounting procedures. Meanwhile, the items themselves will go up or down in market value based on the familiar rules of supply and demand, without regard to what the balance sheet has to say.

This means that if someone sells a 10-year-old tire changer used in his or her auto repair shop, it may bring a figure (perhaps more than hundred dollars) that is much greater than its book value (depreciated down to zero). When all of the assets are turned over to a buyer in the sale of a business, this same dynamic is at work – the sum collected for equipment will most likely exceed, by a substantial sum, what the balance sheet says it is worth. This is recognized as the recapture of depreciation, or a capital gain for the seller.

Among the most difficult of assets to value is the soft asset of goodwill. Many business-es may carry only a token amount assigned to this category on their books. And yet if the company has little left in depreciable hard assets on the balance sheet and sells for a substantial price reflecting its high profitability, there may be little choice but to assign a sizeable portion of the price to the goodwill portion of the purchase.

It's not a favorite for buyers. As a business buyer, you want assets that can be written off (depreciated or amortized) quickly, to enjoy some tax savings in the years ahead. The write off rules for the goodwill asset, however, require a very slow depreciation pace, so buyers can only shelter a small amount of income each year through depreciation of the sum allocated to the goodwill asset in the purchased company.

As if these principles aren't complicated enough, consider the fact that as the seller receives payments on the seller-financed portion of the sales price over a period of years after the deal closes, part of the tax exposure for the business sale will be realized every year during the period that the seller is collecting proceeds.

Part of the challenge is that you may not know what your tax bracket will be in future years, even though you have to do the planning now. This is all the more reason to consult with a tax specialist, ideally, before you remove all the contingencies on your transaction. The time for the seller to conduct this planning, of course, is before the business goes on the market.

Conclusion

How to allocate business assets and what values to place on each can be a most complicated question. Though I've offered a few guidelines here, the ultimate answers need to be obtained from your accountant or tax practitioner. Whether the components of your deal are subject to tax treatment as ordinary income or as a capital item, can make a substantial difference in the final amount of taxes the seller pays on a deal or that the buyer is able to write off in subsequent years.

KEY POINTS FROM THIS CHAPTER

❖ Sellers of businesses who fail to tax plan the way the offering is presented, are at risk of paying more taxes than necessary on the sale of the assets.

❖ It is strongly advised that sellers discuss the allocation of purchase price in their business offerings with a tax attorney, accountant or other tax advisor before the business goes on the market, and certainly before you enter into a sales agreement.

❖ Some general tax planning guidelines are offered so you'll have an overall idea of how the allocation is conducted. But these suggestions are not meant to take the place of the advice provided by your tax expert. He or she is familiar with your situation, and will know how to apply these rules so that you are subject to as little tax exposure as possible.

❖ You should be aware that an allocation favorable to a business seller tends to work against the tax saving interests of the buyer. And visa versa. So the allocation of purchase price, in which the assets for sale are assigned to various categories with different tax consequences, may need to be negotiated between you and the other party.

❖ The seller's agreement to work for a buyer, represented by the post-sale training contract and the covenant not to compete, is considered employment with respect to any income received in return for the work. As such, the values established for these agreements in the allocation of purchase price are subject to taxation as ordinary income, similar to earnings through wages or commissions.

❖ It is in the seller's interests to minimize the amount of the purchase price allocated to the training agreement and covenant not to compete, because they are taxed at the higher rate.

❖ Also subject to taxes, but at a lower rate, are any gains enjoyed by selling assets at a price higher than their value as listed on the business balance sheet (book value). This is commonly what happens in business sales that include an allocation for equipment at say, market value, when the equipment is shown as having a much lower (depreciated) value by the business. The difference between allocated price and depreciated value is the seller's gain, subject to the capital gains tax rate.

❖ Usually it is only the inventory of stock in trade, valued at cost, which is worth, in real and current dollars, exactly the figure assigned to it in the purchase price allocation. This being the case, there would be no tax consequences from the sale of the inventory to the buyer. The seller has neither gained nor lost in this part of the transaction.

❖ Assigning a value to the goodwill of a profitable business can be problematic. If there is little in the way of hard assets, the seller wants to include most of the purchase price in the category of goodwill. The amount by which this figure exceeds the goodwill value on the business's balance sheet may be substantial. And when collected, it will be subject to capital gains taxes. Buyers aren't happy to allocate a great deal of value to goodwill as the write-off rate is very slow.

❖ An additional aspect of a seller's planning – and another reason you must see your tax advisor – concerns the timing of your receipt of the sales proceeds. If you collect all cash at close of escrow, the tax hit is probably going to come in a single year. If you finance for the buyer however, the principal part of your annual income on the note may be apportioned according to the allocation of purchase price. In that case, your planning needs to account, not only for how the allocation has been established, but also what your anticipated earnings from other sources will be during the years you also receive proceeds from the sale of your business.

CHAPTER FIFTEEN

FINANCING THE PURCHASE

At the point in a transaction when it's time to produce the needed funds, the reader may be interested to know about some of the sources for the money that helps in completing the purchase of a small business. And yet the time to begin thinking and planning for this eventuality is not now, but way back toward the beginning of the process.

For the seller, having arranged for a source of cash that is ready to be advanced against the business is astute preparation. You may be glad you conducted this preliminary work, if you get the right buyer in every respect, except that the person is a few thousand dollars short of meeting your price and terms. The difference may come from a lender who has pre-qualified the business for a loan of the down payment or working capital funds. Or it may be your commitment to carry back some of the purchase price with a note paid by the buyer.

Voila! The money awaits and the buyer has all the more reason to believe in the purchase of your business. If the company qualifies for the third party loan, or if you are willing to wait for the rest of your payment over time, it demonstrates to the buyer a measure of confidence in the business. The lender believes in it. The seller is willing to loan on it. The business must represent a sound investment!

And this from the buyer's standpoint: Now, at the precise moment when you want to wrap up a deal, you will see the benefit of those preparatory steps you took some time ago, when you began making arrangements to get a business loan when the time came. Perhaps your readiness to put cash into the deal, will allow you to beat out competitive bids so you can become the new owner of the business you've determined is just right for you.

What happens at this point is merely the process of implementing the preparation that was conducted beforehand, maybe several months before, when the seller "qualified" the business and the buyer obtained an expression of interest from a lender, subject to final review of the deal.

Here are some of these strategies to work on at the beginning of the marketing or the search campaign, or when you're trying to negotiate a deal and need a last- minute cash infusion:

Seller Financing

As you might imagine, the number one source of funding to facilitate the sale of a small business is seller financing. In roughly 60% of the instances of small business sales in nearly every state, some of the money needed to complete the purchase has come from the seller. The standard arrangement is for the buyer to give the seller a cash down payment for whatever amount the parties have agreed on in their negotiations. Typically, a down payment is between one-third and one-half of the purchase price. Then, if the seller is willing to carry the balance, the buyer will issue a promissory note for that amount in favor of the seller. In most cases, the obligation will call for equal monthly payments over an agreed-on period – often three to seven years – to be paid with interest charged on the unpaid balance. Security for this obligation might be the assets of the business only, or a combination of the business and other property owned by the buyer.

I'm a strong advocate of seller financing as I believe it's an important ingredient in the success of a business that has changed hands. As noted, the offering of seller financing when the company is being marketed sends a message to prospective buyers that it must be a solid business with a good future.

In fact, the seller not only is casting a vote of confidence for the business by offering to help finance the deal, but also is demonstrating the intent to stay involved in the fortunes of the business. If someone owes you money on the company you sold, you'll most likely be willing to offer ideas or advice to make sure that company continues to thrive, and can generate the revenues needed for the buyer to pay off the obligation to you.

Seller financing, of course, can take several forms and need not constitute the entire balance of the purchase price, after the down payment. I've been involved in transactions that used seller financing with some adjustments on the usual theme in order to accommodate the circumstances of the purchase. In one variation, the seller may wait three or six months before the payments begin. This gives the buyer an opportunity to get both feet on the ground in the company, to take care of any unexpected cash requirements (there always seem to be a few of those), and to put a few dollars into building up the business. Another alternative is for the seller to receive proceeds due on the note in one or more balloon payments, rather than in monthly installments. This plan works well in a situation where a buyer intends to obtain other financing on the business, or to use different means to raise the funds within a year or so of the transfer. In effect, this tactic is calling on the seller to provide a swing loan – some money to tide the buyer over and complete the purchase – until arrangements can be made for more permanent financing. The seller in this example is not actually giving funds to the buyer, but is postponing collection of money owed, earning some interest on it and giving the buyer time to get the funds needed to retire or pay down the debt to the seller.

I've also seen seller financing structured with more than one note issued by a buyer in favor of the seller. This strategy combines standard seller financing—using a note paid in monthly installments over an agree-on period of years, and a note due to be retired in six or 12 months. And in one case I know about, in which the seller took a note from a buyer who planned to build up the business for resale, the parties agreed the note would be paid off with accrued interest upon the next sale of the business, whenever that might be.

Along with help financing purchase of the business, the seller often provides other benefits to the buyer, including: the offer of advice if needed (hoping to insure that the business will survive and the note will be paid), flexibility about terms of the deal, and sometimes granting a below-market interest rate to make the deal.

While some consultants advise sellers to get every scrap of collateral available when carrying back financing for the buyer, others feel that asking for security beyond the business itself is likely to discourage a buyer from wanting to deal.

My thought is that the way to collateralize such a loan is dependent on a number of factors. If there is a substantial down payment in relation to the size of the obligation to the seller, it probably is unnecessary to collateralize the buyer's note on the remaining sum – besides assets of the business. That's certainly the case if there is enough value in the business assets – equipment, receivables and inventory – to support the amount due.

A highly leveraged deal, however, is a blueprint for disaster if the buyer can't make the business successful enough to support the debt load. If you're a seller whose deal is shaping up in a way that leaves you feeling vulnerable to loss in the event the business goes under, then don't agree to the proposal unless and until the obligation is backed up with the pledge of other security, such as real estate.

And you can be flexible in this area as well. Parts of the collateral can be released over the period of an obligation as it becomes "seasoned." In one case, a five year note was initially secured by the business as well as the buyer's real property. After 18 months of prompt payments on the obligation, it was rewritten to require only the business assets as collateral. I believe this arrangement was needlessly complicated, but it made a deal possible for parties who were split on the issue of using the real estate security for the note. This was the compromise both could accept.

If you, as a seller, are willing to help finance the purchase of your business, and to be flexible as to how that is done, you will increase the chances of finding a buyer willing and able to meet your other terms.

And from the standpoint of the buyer, your best source of financing is the seller of the business, I advocate that you work with your seller to find an arrangement that makes you both feel comfortable, allowing you to borrow some of your purchase price from the person who knows the business best.

The Cheapest Conventional Money

While seller financing is likely the best deal a buyer can get on funds needed to complete a purchase, the least costly loan from a conventional source is usually the home equity line offered by many banks and savings and loan institutions.

I particularly like the idea of borrowing on home equity, not only because the rates beat business loans, but also because the real estate lending route involves less red tape, requires less reporting and usually gets approved and funded more quickly than most kinds of business loans. If a buyer has real estate with a value exceeding its mortgages, and a fairly good credit record, there are dozens of financial institutions ready to provide the cash for whatever purpose the borrower wishes to put it.

There's nothing you as a seller can do to facilitate your buyer getting this kind of a loan, because it's not related to the company – your business pre-approval work would not be relevant. But you may want to recommend this approach if your buyer hasn't thought about it and has real property equity.

Many buyers reject this idea because they think simply that they ought to get a business loan to accomplish business purposes. In the case of most loans to purchase a business, however, the borrower is required to put up real property equity as collateral. That's right: When a business bank is called on to lend capital that will go into the down payment on a small company, the borrower is probably going to be asked to put up a second trust deed in the family home, so the lender is protected in the event the business is unable to provide the money needed to service the loan.

It doesn't take a shrewd business mind to figure out that if your real estate equity needs to be pledged anyway, you might as well get regular home equity money with the lower rates and all the other borrower benefits that come with it.

Bizbuyfinancing.com

For many business buyers, the most logical source of funding to complete a purchase is accessed on the Internet at *www.bizbuyfinancing.com* Offering a direct connection to lenders who specialize in business purchase loans, along with timely advice, help with pre-qualification, a loan payment calculator and other useful tools, this web site should be visited by those who anticipate the need for financial assistance to buy a small business and want useful information as well as competitive rates from experienced business lenders.

And sellers looking for an effective resource at which to get financing pre-approval, should make sure to visit the *www.bizbuyfinancing.com* site.

SBA Guaranteed

Among the most common institutional sources of money for a business acquisition is represented by the network of lenders backed by the SBA (U.S. Small Business Administration). The federal agency will guarantee loans made for purchasing a company, or other business needs, for enterprises that comply with its small business definition (up to 500 employees for most companies in manufacturing, a maximum of 100 employees in wholesale trades, a lid on annual revenues – averaged over a three-year period – of $6 million for most firms in retail and service industries, $28.5 million for the majority of businesses involved in general and heavy construction, and $12 million for special trade contractors.) A benefit of this program is that borrowers without real estate for collateral still can meet the government agency's qualifications. And with this approval, many institutions will ratify loan requests up to $250,000. But if there are real estate or other available assets in the borrower's portfolio, besides the business, the lenders usually insist on using such assets – up to the value of the loan – as additional security.

What the SBA looks at are four key factors, and at least three of the four should be present for a buyer to qualify with a lender who'll seek the SBA guarantee, and therefore will be more likely to provide for a business need than will a conventional bank. The factors are: 1. Cash flow of the business; 2. Borrower's work experience as it relates to the business; 3. Borrower's credit history; and 4. Collateral of the borrower, in addition to the business assets, that can be used to secure the obligation.

The well prepared seller, anticipating the possibility of an SBA approved buyer, can build some financing for both a down payment and working capital right into the offering of the business.

And sellers can assemble part of the SBA package – the portion that requires a narrative and financial history of your business – for a buyer who may want this kind of loan for some of the purchase money. The buyer's contribution to the application for an SBA guaranteed loan will be to include his or her work history, a business plan, credit check approval and related documents.

Business Assets Lending

Money also is available from some business lenders who will take the company's liquid assets as collateral. It's common for owners of established retail firms to use inventory financing. The money helps them stock up for the holiday selling season, for example. And the inventory either is pledged to the lender to make sure the loan will be retired, or is signed over to the lender, and then released in increments back to the borrower, in return for progress payments.

Receivables financing is another way of using liquid assets to raise capital. Owners of many distribution and manufacturing businesses find that although the company is enjoying good revenues with satisfactory profit margins, most of the earnings are tied up in receivables. Until customers pay their bills, the business might be strapped for the cash needed to expand production, modernize facilities or market more aggressively. One way to improve cash flow in this situation is to pledge the receivables to a business lender for a loan of up to 80% of the value of those receivables. As the company collects the funds owed to it, the loan balance is paid down. And some firms are able to pass along to their slow-paying customers, their cost of borrowing in the form of a finance charge.

A variation on this idea is for the company to sell its receivables to a factor – someone who'll pay somewhere between 60% and 80% of the face receivables value, and then will be responsible for getting customers to pay up.

These are fairly common practices used by established businesses with existing lender relationships to ease occasional cash crunches. But there's no reason a buyer and seller can't ask a business bank to put up some of the money that will be used for the purchase of the company, and to accept the company's liquid assets for collateral. Inventory or receivables loans may not generate as much cash as a typical SBA-backed lending deal. But for part of a purchase price or for working capital, this may be an ideal source.

If you are completing the purchase of a business, an appropriate choice of a bank might be the one now serving that business. Ask your seller to tell his or her contact at the company's bank that you will be its new customer if it can help make the deal with a loan secured by the business' liquid assets.

And from the viewpoint of the seller, this strategy represents another opportunity for you to do some valuable preparatory work before you start marketing the business: Tell your current bank that your company will probably continue to be a customer, under its new ownership, if the bank can help make the deal with a loan secured by the business' liquid assets.

Innovative Financing Strategies for Buyers

As the owner of a small business, you'll be confronted with challenges which are best met using resourceful planning and creative problem solving. You may get the chance to begin developing those skills if you're trying to complete a purchase, need a little more cash to accomplish that goal, and find the money is not available from the usual sources.

These strategies also should be considered by business sellers who can recommend them to their buyers, and in some cases, help the buyer with implementation.

An important possible resource is found in the list of the business' vendors – the organizations supplying the company with the products, materials and services that enable it to function. If suppliers would like to keep doing business with the company under its new ownership, perhaps they'll be willing to stretch out the period during which they usually require their bills to be paid.

If a corner grocery is changing hands, ask the wholesaler providing much of the inventory whether they can wait 45, instead of 15 days to get paid for package and dairy goods. That concession will give the new owner of the business a little extra money for working capital needs, so he or she can dig deeper into current cash reserves to meet the down payment request.

A variation on this plan is for one or more of the vendors to let the buyer pay some of the old bills. If it's a photo lab changing hands, for example, and it owes $25,000 to an outfit that handles some of its high resolution scanning and digitizing work, find out if the buyer can take on this responsibility in the seller's place. What about extending the terms of payment? If so, that's another $25,000 the seller doesn't need right away (to clear up payables) and it can be used by the purchaser to build up business.

Traditionally, vendors are reluctant to extend credit for new business operators, but since the end of the dot-com economy, many companies are re-thinking their stances on this and other practices, making this an idea worth exploring.

A completely different approach is for the buyer to use a provision of tax law that allows the rollover of IRA or 401K funds into a trust, and permitting funds in the trust to be used for purchase of a business without liability for deferred taxes. In other words, if the buyer has tax protected retirement money in mutual funds or other investments, he or she may think that the deferred tax bill will have to be paid if the money is used for a less passive investment. Not so. A provision of the U.S. Tax Code recognizes the rollover of invested funds into a business opportunity as a transaction that does not interfere with the deferred status of the taxpayer's money. This is a strategy that may make it possible for the buyer to "find" several thousand more dollars to put into the purchase.

If none of these approaches will yield enough for the needed down payment, how about putting the amount of the shortfall into a promissory note, which the seller can then discount and sell in a few months to get his or her cash? For sake of discussion, let's assume that the buyer can provide $150,000 of the $200,000 down payment requested. Where will the other $50,000 come from? The strategy suggested here, is that the seller takes that money in the form of the note and then, after the note has had a chance to "season" – with all payments made promptly for six or nine months – the seller would ask a note "buy-back" company to take over as the creditor in return for the going rate – probably 80% ($40,000) for the "paper." This enables the seller to get most of the down payment; there's just a wait involved to collect the part that wasn't available when the deal closed.

One of the nice aspects of this plan is that the seller doesn't have to wait till months after the deal closes, to find out if this can work, hoping the whole time to be able to find someone to buy back the note. This is one of the areas in which the seller can do some planning when preparing the business for sale.

By contacting organizations which buy back promissory notes of this type, the seller can work toward an understanding about what size note can be sold and at what discount rate. Additionally, the seller can prepare the business-assets side of this under-standing. Provide the buy-back organization with the information needed so the business can be pre-approved for the note purchase. At the same time, the seller can find out what qualifications will be required of a buyer – the person who will make payments to the note holder once it is sold. That means a buyer with insufficient cash but a good credit rating and, perhaps, other assets, might be qualified to purchase your business.

And if all else fails, there's one other source of capital which – though I consider it to be the "bank of last resort" – is commonly used by small business buyers and owners to raise money, fast. It involves a plea to the friendly lenders who fill our mail boxes with Visa and Master Card offers. Keep this in mind when buyer and seller think there is no other place to get that last $10,000 or $20,000 needed to close the deal – most likely there is.

Credit card borrowing comes at a high interest rate to be sure, but if the sum standing between the buyer and the business can be accessed easily with the plastic in the buyer's wallet – and he or she is motivated to take over the company – it's a strategy well worth considering.

A Note of Caution

After reviewing these suggestions about ways for a buyer to incur additional debt to come up with all the cash requested by the seller, the reader may be reminded of the candidates for political office who pledge to expand services while cutting taxes. The question to ask is: If the buyer is going to incur all these obligations, where will the money come from to pay them? In fact, both buyer and seller might want to take a pencil and paper to the problem so as to determine if the business cash flow realistically can incur all of these obligations.

Just how much debt do you think the business will be able to reasonably support? For the first several months after the buyer takes over, there probably will not be the same level of cash coming from the enterprise as was enjoyed by the seller, particularly considering the deposits and start-up expenses that will pop up in the early months of the new ownership. And then there is the cost of the mistakes a new owner is bound to make while learning the business.

If the seller has a firm grasp of reality, he or she will not encourage the buyer to try and pull off a highly leveraged deal on the purchase of the company. The seller stands to lose as much as the buyer if the company can't continue to function in a productive condition.

Whether the business that has changed hands is making money or barely generating enough to meet operating costs, the odds are against a buyer succeeding at building it up, even keeping it going, if there is insufficient cash. In many cases the over-leveraged deal results in the company collapsing under the weight of its own debt. If the business is over encumbered and under performing, the buyer has, at risk, the down payment, personal assets and the time that will be invested in this project. The seller's risks include the amount which he or she financed, and the possibility of being hauled into court by a disgruntled buyer who seeks to recover some or all of what was invested.

Certainly buyers and sellers should explore all avenues for raising money so as to complete the deal. But these ideas should be tempered with the good judgment about the possibilities of loss and the risks the parties are willing to take.

Shared Equity

One final strategy can work out well if the buyer is not prepared to acquire the business all at once, but there is a bond of trust between the parties. The two can form a partnership or a corporation in which the buyer takes over some or most of the ownership, conducts most of the work and assumes most of the responsibility. The seller can stay on as a partner, take an appropriate salary and work with the buyer who completes the purchase over time, as more money is generated from the business and is provided to the seller to pay for the buyer's growing stake.

There are any number of ways to structure such a deal, and plenty of attorneys, bankers, insurance agents (who will arrange to underwrite a buy/sell agreement triggered by the death or illness of buyer or seller), and other consultants who can help you make this happen. That's really the easy part.

The critical question is whether there is enough trust and communication between the buyer and the seller to make this work.

This strategy is not, of course, as easy and quick as an outright purchase. But if there is a solid connection between the parties and you really want to enter into a transaction, even if it takes some time to complete, the two of you should explore the idea of "sharing" the company for awhile.

Conclusion

Preparation of a small business for sale cannot be complete unless the seller has explored some of the ways to source additional capital that may be needed to close a deal. And the buyer's preparatory work should include lining up the cash sources that will help when it comes time to complete the deal. I encourage sellers to be the bank, to the extent possible, so both parties have a stake in the business' continuing success. But this isn't an ideal world. So parties are well advised to do some back-up planning by determining where the extra funds might come from. The seller frequently can get the business pre-approved by possible lenders so that when the time comes to raise the funds, some of the work is completed, and the process can proceed quickly.

Among the suggestions offered are the traditional resources for business capital including SBA secured money, cash advanced on liquid assets of the business and – perhaps surprisingly – a simple home equity loan. Another good resource is found at *www.bizbuyfinancing.com* Less traditional techniques include tapping vendors for extensions on the time needed for the business to discharge its accounts payables, and rolling over retirement accounts into tax-protected trusts that can help fund a business. Another strategy for getting money involves arranging a pre-approval on the business, which will later help sell a somewhat "seasoned" note from a buyer to a note buy-back service. The buyer also can yield to the call of the banks that want to offer cash and lines of credit accessed through their Visa and MasterCard accounts. Also discussed is the approach that uses equity in the company rather that debt to accommodate a buyer whom the seller particularly likes.

KEY POINTS FROM THIS CHAPTER

❖ *The number one source of funding to facilitate the sale of a small business – accounting for about 60% of the deals – is seller financing of at least some of the money needed.*

❖ *Seller financing offers a number of advantages in the way it adds to the appeal of the business. And it usually provides affordable purchase money for the buyer.*

❖ *The question of whether to collateralize the note to the seller with business assets only, or with other property of the buyer, is often a point for negotiation when seller financing is involved. There is no single right solution for this matter and sellers are advised to eliminate their risks as much as possible, without putting an excessive burden on the buyer.*

❖ *For many business buyers the best resource for additional money for completing a purchase, in addition to useful information and other valuable online finance tools, can be found at www.bizbuyfinancing.com*

❖ *And sellers can go to www.bizbuyfinancing.com to find out about getting the business pre-approved for an acquisition loan.*

❖ *The cheapest conventional way to borrow is usually with a home equity loan – a preferable deal to most loan packages granted to buy a business. The later come with higher interest rates and more qualifying and reporting requirements, along with the need to put up real estate as additional collateral.*

❖ *One approach to getting an institutional loan for a business purchase, without real estate security, is the program offered by the Federal Government through the SBA. It guarantees business loans from select institutions to those who qualify.*

❖ *Lenders who provide receivables or inventory financing might be resources for some of the cash needed to complete the sale of a small business.*

❖ *Another way to raise money for the seller's down payment is to pre-qualify the business with a service that buys back promissory notes. The seller can discount and sell a note received from the buyer after six or nine months of "seasoning."*

❖ *Vendors to the business can be a source of financing if they will agree to let the buyer take responsibility for the seller's payables. This strategy frees up cash that may not have to go into the down payment, but can be used for working capital. Vendors also can cooperate with the new buyer by permitting an extension in payment of their obligations.*

❖ *Parties to a small business sale might like to know a buyer can roll over his or her retirement account into a trust that can be used to buy a business without triggering any immediate tax consequences*

❖ *The "bank of last resort," using credit cards, is sometimes the solution for a buyer who needs more cash to complete a deal and has no other resources.*

❖ *Sellers often can help their buyers find more money but should be aware of the dangers of overburdening a business with financial obligations. And buyers need to do some cash flow planning to make sure they'll have a manageable level of debt when taking over a small business.*

❖ *If a buyer can't raise enough money through increased debt to buy all of a business, one solution is to buy part or most of the business and become partners or a corporate shareholder with the seller.*

CHAPTER SIXTEEN

DUE DILIGENCE

Imagine going to all the effort to investigate and consider dozens of businesses for sale, finally discovering one that you want, engaging in difficult negotiations until you hammer out a deal, then getting close to completing your purchase, only to have the transaction self-destruct at the last minute.

Or if you're the seller, how would you feel after you've marketed your business for months, located a strong, interested buyer who goes through weeks of hard bargaining until an agreement is reached, but a few days before the escrow is to be completed, you learn that your buyer has pulled the lever for the escape hatch and has decided not to remove the last of the contingencies, which means there will be no transaction after all?

These unpleasant experiences describe roughly half of the deals which start out with a signed purchase/sale agreement, but don't stay alive long enough to reach completion.

Why Half the Deals Fail

This means that even if you've got a ratified agreement to purchase or to sell a small business, there only is a 50/50 chance you'll be able to close. The deal killer may well be your inability to get the approval of a third party needed to proceed toward completion. And if the landlord or franchisor or other third party is in agreement with the intended deal, the problem may be that the information disclosed during the early introduction between the possible buyer and the business, does not correspond with what is discovered during the due diligence period.

These two factors account for most of the reasons that transactions run off their tracks before completion. And what's most disturbing about these deal killers is that they usually are preventable, or at least the problems can be foreseen long before parties have invested a great deal of time and professional fees in their effort to complete a transaction.

If the seller isn't going to get the cooperation needed from key business relations – in most cases it's the landlord and/or franchisor – there is little likelihood of selling the business. And that's a fact of life that should be established before undertaking a marketing effort.

As to the prevention of a deal "meltdown" caused by mis-statements, the solution is simple: The buyer is honest about his or her financial and management capabilities from the first introduction, and the seller makes certain that any statements about the business – whether in verbal or written form – can be supported with the evidence, such as the company's financial records.

There have been circumstances I've witnessed where the business, when subjected to a due diligence examination, proved to be doing even better than the seller said. And that's a happy surprise. But in most cases that's not what happens.

I'm reminded of a young man – Larry – who worked in bicycle shops from the time he was in high school, dreaming of one day owning his own. He had definite plans for what he wanted to do – what products he wanted to offer, what repair services he wanted to feature and how he wanted to promote the business. He'd been disappointed when the bicycle store in which he worked, and thought he could buy, was sold to the owner's relative instead.

Larry then launched a campaign to find a store he could purchase with the money he'd saved and a cash gift promised by his grandmother. After a few months he entered into a deal for a long-established bicycle retail and repair business and was nearly ecstatic about the impending close of escrow. He had just enough money for the required down payment and a bit of working capital, and he would then make payments for the balance owed to the seller out of his earnings from the business.

During the due diligence examination however, Larry was disappointed to notice that the shop's tax returns and bank statements told a different story about the revenues and earnings than did the seller when they first had talked.

When Larry pointed out the discrepancies, the seller's answer was that since Larry was not an accountant, he was not qualified to understand the business records. So Larry hired an accountant who reviewed the same information and came to the same conclusion.

Larry did not know what to do. He really wanted to buy the shop, but the accountant told him that it was not generating enough income to allow for the payments to the seller and for an income. Was Larry willing to work for free for a couple of years?

In their final conversation, the seller told Larry that it was only the checks and credit card receipts which were noted in the business records. All of the cash transactions were "off the books." The seller encouraged Larry to go through with the deal, assuring him that he'd make enough money.

Since the due diligence examination of the business records was a contingency of their agreement, Larry could back out of the deal if he wasn't satisfied. He spent a sleepless night debating with himself about the correct action.

Larry made the decision to ask for his deposit back and to continue looking for a bicycle business to buy; he hoped it would be from someone more forthright than the last seller with whom he'd dealt.

It's often the case that the buyer will begin to imagine himself or herself in charge of the business, and is hoping during due diligence examination, that everything will work out as anticipated. But it's a good idea not to order the company's new stationery just yet. I advise buyers not to allow that enthusiasm to cloud your clear thinking. As much as you, the prospective buyer, like and trust the seller, make sure that whatever information you are provided as part of your due diligence investigation is consistent with your expectations. You don't want surprises at this point. Your agreement with the seller should include a contingency for your satisfactory review of the business financials and the other details you want to analyze. If the unexpected happens – the business does not prove to be as profitable or as trouble-free as you were led to believe – be prepared to exercise your right to decline moving forward on the deal.

In fact, I recommend to buyers that they keep one eye open for other opportunities, even as they are conducting due diligence on a small business they plan to buy. The seller will likely be taking back-up offers in case you don't work out as the buyer. There's no reason you shouldn't be aware of other offerings while you're checking out the business you have on contract.

Should an Accountant Get Involved?

To aid the buyer in due diligence examination, it might be wise to engage the services of an accountant. The professional's job will be to review the financial records of the company and determine if the broker and the seller made accurate and truthful statements when they quoted the figures for the company's revenues and the owner's income. After all, it is these statements that the buyer has relied on to decide whether, and at what price to purchase the business.

Some buyers feel they can handle the due diligence review of the financials without aid of a paid professional. The individual's investigation will involve matching documentation of sales, such as customer invoices and cash register receipts, with bank deposits. And it's useful to compare items in the expense ledger of the P & L with the check book and invoices from suppliers.

Much of this work involves just the tedious application of simple math. And the buyer who is competent with figures and is seeking to save some money might consider this a do-it-yourself project. Be aware, however, that there are a number of accounting procedures and practices with which you may not be familiar. It's easy to get confused when items are credited to one account and a corresponding debit needs to be entered to maintain the "balance" in the company's balance sheet.

Besides, there are ways to make a company look more profitable than it really is. If the prospective buyer is not familiar with some of the more sophisticated accounting techniques, it might make sense to pay the fee for a competent professional to go over the records. He or she will know what to look for and will spot inconsistencies by which the information is not complete and accurate. And if there are questions about how the seller keeps track of certain items and reports on various categories of income and expenses, the professional will be able to ferret out the needed information and understand what is going on.

I've observed how buyers conducting due diligence can become confused and intimidated when the seller's CPA responds to their questions with complicated technical explanations. No need for that if the buyer is represented by an accounting professional who can talk the same language.

Other Due Diligence Tasks

In addition to the books and records, of course, there are other items the buyer should inspect and learn about during the period of due diligence. I think it's a good idea to see samples of the company's promotion and advertising efforts, and check out the firm's handbook, if there is one. That provides insight into the rules for employees and the standard practices that are followed in the company.

The seller should be asked, at this point, to disclose information on any lawsuits in which the business was involved during the past five years. It's not important to know about the particulars of a specific action, but I would be concerned if a company has a history of being sued or of having to go to court to collect its receivables.

The seller's concerns about confidentiality may make it difficult for a buyer to spend much time at the premises during business hours, as that might alert employees that something is going on. If the possible buyer can manage to drop by for a few minutes in the guise of a customer or as a vendor, he or she should be as observant as possible. Do the employees seem productive? Is the phone ringing? What's the mood of the place – energetic and active, or slow and somber?

I'm not an advocate of fabricating stories, even to accomplish the covert mission of checking out the business. So I think it's a better cover for the buyer to be introduced as a possible investor or as a friend of the owner – both of which are somewhat factual, rather than coming into the place of business with some elaborate falsification about auditing the books or conducting an insurance investigation.

This delicate matter was handled intelligently by a manufacturer's representative for consumer products lines, who took a few prospective buyers of her business to meet some account contacts. The seller wasn't ready to tell her customers – mostly department store fashion accessory buyers – that she was selling the business, but didn't feel it would be right to make up some outrageous story. So clients were told the person accompanying the rep was a possible new employee for her company. Once a buyer was secured, following an accepted offer and then a completed escrow, the customers were told that the person was going to be taking over the business. The seller felt the approach was appropriate because it put her customers on notice that she was in the process of making some changes, without getting into the details of what was being changed – the company's ownership.

While the buyer is checking out the company, other things to look at are the business' existing contracts with customers or employees, insurance policies, vendor agreements and any other documents relevant to the business. If these agreements are transferred, the new owner will be responsible to perform on them and will reap their benefits. It's best to find out what's involved, so the buyer can make sure he or she is in agreement.

This also is the time for the buyer to learn some of the things he or she needs to know about the industry in which the company functions, and whether it is growing or declining. What are prospects for the future of the area in which the company is located? This is particularly important if the business is a retail company that depends on locals with discretionary income for its survival.

Seller's Due Diligence Role

In addition to verifying the information provided by the buyer – does he or she have the cash and a good credit rating as was represented? – the seller should plan to get involved with the buyer's due diligence examination.

The buyer may have a number of questions about the operation of the company, and the seller needs to be prepared to provide assistance in any way possible, as the soon-to-be new owner works out the beginnings of a relationship with the landlord, tries to make sense of the financials, looks at the advertising and promotional materials, pours through invoices, customer orders, payroll records and the business check register.

This is not the time for a seller to relax. I can recall deals that went bad in the eleventh hour because the seller was not actively engaged in making sure of the buyer's progress during the important process of due diligence. In one situation, a seller took a little celebratory vacation – a bit prematurely it turned out – leaving the buyer alone with the business information at the office of the seller's accountant.

In walked the seller's former partner, a man with whom the seller had experienced a serious falling out years before. This former partner had gone on to become involved in other enterprises, failing at each one, and continuing to carry a grudge against the seller, as well as many other people with whom he'd been involved.

In fact, the former partner did not get along well with others, and besides, was not a trustworthy individual. But the buyer had no way of knowing that. And after the buyer spent the afternoon hearing angry criticism of the seller coming from the former partner, the buyer concluded he wanted to no part of the deal. When the seller returned to town, he learned that the buyer had rescinded his agreement to purchase the business.

The seller later learned what had occurred and considered suing the former partner for the damage – he'd lost a sale – resulting from the slander. Ultimately the seller concluded it was his own fault for not being present while the buyer was learning about the business.

My advice to sellers is to be involved at every step of the buyer's due diligence, including meetings with landlords, key vendors and anyone else whom the buyer feels should be contacted while the business is under scrutiny. This is certainly what brokers do to make sure a deal is going to work. After all, if you've reached the point of achieving an accepted offer on your business, you are approaching your goal. This is no time to cut back on your efforts.

Conclusion

When it's time for the due diligence portion of a transaction, both buyers and sellers should be aware that half of the accepted offers on small businesses do not result in successfully concluded transactions. Frequently, the problem can be attributed either to the failure of a key third party to cooperate, or to a buyer's discovery that the offering doesn't live up to the way it was advertised.

The seller can guard against such problems by making sure – before the business is offered for sale – that key third parties, such as landlord and franchisor, are prepared to cooperate with a sale. And if buyer and seller are careful not to make exaggerations, misrepresentations or promises that can't be fulfilled when dealing with the other party, there is less likelihood the deal will self-destruct when the period of due diligence is being conducted.

The buyer is advised that there are benefits and disadvantages to conducting the financial due diligence on a do-it-yourself basis; it helps if you have some skill and experience in analyzing company records. Otherwise, it's smart to bring in an accounting professional.

Other due diligence tasks include observing the business – though that can be difficult in light of the need for confidentiality – and studying agreements the company has with customers, employees and vendors.

And sellers are advised to stay involved with the buyer during the due diligence part of the transaction. This is no time to relax.

KEY POINTS FROM THIS CHAPTER

❖ *You have a 50/50 chance, statistically, of successfully completing a purchase following an accepted offer. That's primarily because businesses don't always stand up to inspections, and because the approvals and clearances needed for change of ownership are not always forthcoming.*

❖ *While the buyer doesn't have control over the circumstances of the business – it's up to the seller to relay all the facts, correctly, and be ready to support statements with proof – the buyer can uphold his or her end of the agreement by making sure that financial abilities and work experience are accurately represented.*

❖ *Just as a smart seller takes back up offers – even when there is a ratified deal in progress, the buyer is well advised to keep looking at other opportunities during the due diligence review on a business which the buyer has a contract to buy.*

❖ *Engaging an accountant to conduct the due diligence financial analysis is probably the surest way to learn quickly if the company does enough profitable business to reward the buyer for his or her efforts, and to help retire the debt taken on to make the purchase.*

❖ *Some buyers want to take care of examining the books and records yourself, and not work with an accountant. The major benefit – saving the fee that would be spent for the professional's work – may not be worth the risk of being misled about the financial performance of the company, unless you have the skills and knowledge of an accounting professional.*

❖ *Buyers are advised not to stop at financial information when conducting due diligent examination of a prospective business to buy. Make sure to view the contracts with employees, vendors and customers and other agreements important to the company's operation.*

❖ *Other things to inform yourself about, if you are conducting due diligence on a company to buy, are prior lawsuits, trends in the industry and changes in the geographic area where the company conducts business.*

❖ *The smart seller stays closely in touch with the buyer involved in the due diligence process. This is no time for the seller to run the risk that a little problem might ruin a deal after all the work and time invested in getting this far.*

CHAPTER SEVENTEEN

CLOSING YOUR DEAL

If you remember the scenes from movies taking place in the Old West, you might recall that when two gamblers had a bet going they engaged a stakeholder to hang onto the cash that each put up and then pass the whole kitty over to the one who drew the most aces, or fired the most silver dollars out of the air with his six shooter, or whatever the bet. Or the middleman in a horse sale took responsibility for making sure that the seller showed up with the designated stallion and that the buyer brought all the money agreed on.

The job of stakeholder pretty much describes one of the key assignments of escrow services or escrow attorneys hired to handle the documents and the money involved in the transfer of small businesses in the 21st Century. But things have become a bit more complex since then, so the escrow service has much more to do than just stuff the cash in one blue jeans' pocket and the business ownership certificate in the other.

Operating in most every state, a business escrow service provides the vital functions that will allow you to close your deal according to the rules of the state in which you are operating. These rules are set up to make sure a business owner can't sell off the company without paying what's owed to employees, taxing authorities, vendors and those who might have a lien on equipment used in the business.

For buyers of a small business, the protection offered by these procedures is obvious: You won't receive a nasty surprise to the effect that your new business comes with hidden obligations and undisclosed debt.

And if you're a seller, the benefit of following these rules is the protection from anyone who attempts to establish that you have liabilities beyond what was declared and substantiated as part of the transfer. And that means there's little likelihood you can be sued or subjected to other legal actions resulting from the sale.

Opening the Escrow

The first thing you and the other party will do when working with the stakeholder is to furnish the facts about the terms of your deal and to provide instructions to the service. You can anticipate a fee for the escrow company of at least a few hundred dollars, for a simple transaction with few services required, up to several thousand dollars, if it is a large transaction and there is a need for several documents to be prepared.

Ordinarily the fees are split 50/50 between buyer and seller and the escrow firm will probably want some of the money at the beginning. You also will be asked to sign some documents to get things started.

And here are some of the things with which the escrow service will be involved:

Lien search

A check of the public records is made to determine the rightful owner of the company's equipment and fixtures, and if there are any claims on them. Similar to a title search conducted on real property, this procedure is meant to find out if there are any liens on the personal property used in the business. The search is managed by accessing records for property under the name of the business, or its address, or name of the owner. Or all three. It's not unusual to discover that a prior owner or some taxing authority has neglected to remove a lien or claim that has long since been satisfied. And part of the escrow service's job will be to track down the parties and paperwork to verify that the items being sold are free of any encumbrances.

If there are existing liens, they would ordinarily be paid by the seller. Or, it's possible to work out an arrangement whereby the buyer takes the assets "subject to" those liens. Any financial obligations of the seller arising from such encumbrances could be assumed by the buyer as part of the negotiations. In most cases, the lien holder – the party who has an interest in the property – will have to agree to the transfer from seller to buyer. And there are various ways to work with this requirement.

Liens that can and should be resolved are handled as part of the escrow process. If the seller needs to pay off obligations for the removal of the liens, the escrow service might arrange to do that at the close of the transaction, using some of the funds paid in by the buyer and meant to be credited to the seller's account.

Receiving claims

The escrow holder will hear from anyone who feels they have a claim or interest in the business or any of the property of the business. These will be the responsibility of the seller to handle – either by demonstrating that the claims are not valid or by instructing the escrow holder to pay them. Among the notifications received by escrow, there are likely to be requests from government taxing authorities which enter claims as a matter of course, just to make sure no one is able to close a deal without being current with their obligations.

The escrow service will review and pass along to the seller any claims that come in. The buyer may or may not be informed about these items. It's usually not critical that the buyer is up to date on the seller's obligation unless he or she will be assuming some of them as part of the structure of the deal.

Notice of impending sale

Though parties usually want to keep their deal quiet as possible until it takes effect, they are required in most states to publish a notice about the impending change in ownership for the business. Usually these notices are published in a general circulation newspaper in the area. If the business is involved in the sale of alcoholic beverages either in packages (such as a liquor or grocery store), or by the drink (as in a restaurant or bar), an additional notice may be required to alert the public of a change of ownership for the liquor license.

By complying with this requirement for a public notice, the parties to a deal and their escrow service are effectively notifying any creditors of the intent to transfer business assets. With this procedure, any interested taxing authorities, banks and other lenders, equipment suppliers and vendors are provided legal notice about the transaction planned. The notice provides them with a certain number of days to contact the escrow company so they can enter their claims.

It's incumbent on potential creditors to become informed about any transfers involving property in which they may have an interest. That's why most companies and governmental agencies have someone in the accounts receivables and lending departments who is charged with the job of following all the legal notices. These people quickly contact any escrow services handling property in which their organization has an interest.

Requesting releases

Even if no taxing authorities have entered a claim, the escrow services usually request clearances from the relevant Federal, State and local tax agencies, just to make sure that the seller is up to date in paying taxes due on sales, payroll, personal property assessments and income.

Verifying approvals

A similar procedure to requesting releases is the escrow's job to contact a landlord for a business being transferred, to confirm the details provided about the lease transfer. And, with the landlord's okay, the escrow can help in this activity by keeping track of the new lease or lease assignment, getting it signed by the parties and delivering copies at close of escrow. If the buyer will operate with the seller's current lease, any prorations needed will be handled between buyer and the seller in escrow. If a new lease is involved, with added payments due to the landlord, the escrow service may include the landlord in this part of the procedure, having him sign relevant documents and providing him a check for any added rental deposit and/or increased rent.

Approvals needed from institutional or non-institutional lenders also can be verified by the escrow holder. And escrow will make sure any necessary funds to be loaned the buyer are ready when needed, and that loan papers have been properly presented and, at the closing, are signed.

Preparing documents

The loan payments made by the buyer to the seller will need a promissory note to be official, and that is a document which the escrow ordinarily drafts for both, using standard language, and inserting the names of the parties, terms of the loan and a reference to any other documents (in many states it is a "security agreement") which list the assets that are used to secure the obligation. Also prepared by the escrow service can be the other parts of your agreement, such as the covenant not to compete, the training contract and any other deals the buyer and seller have made to facilitate the transaction.

Waiting it Out

After these tasks are completed, there may be a lull in activity as you and the other party to the deal wait for expiration of the mandatory periods associated with the published notices. The seller should focus on making sure the business is running smoothly and the buyer will be busy with preparatory tasks, such as applying with the local government recorder to use the business name, setting up a bank account and, perhaps, getting started on a business plan.

And there are a couple of other things parties can keep in mind as the clock ticks toward the day when the transfer will be complete. One is to maintain the confidentiality about the impending sale. Indeed, it may be hard to keep the secret at this point; a number of people may have been brought in on the "secret," such as the landlord, vendors who are planning to work with the buyer for special finance arrangements, and perhaps an employee or two who were taken into your confidence early in the process and sworn to secrecy in return for the seller's promise of an incentive once the deal closes. But I advocate keeping the information as quiet as possible. In the event something was to go wrong and disrupt your sale, you'd have a lot of explaining to do, not to mention your state of embarrassment.

I realize that it's hard to keep quiet a fact that has become a matter of public record with publishing in the newspaper. Most of the customers and employees probably are not reading the legal notices however, and you should make every effort not to talk about the sale.

If there is a liquor license involved and your state requires a notice of license transfer to be plastered to the front window of the business, this will be hard to ignore. And so you will want to be ready with an explanation for anyone who asks. It's best to tell the truth, but be as succinct about it as possible, sparing others the details of your deal. You still aren't 100% sure it'll happen and you don't want to go into more excruciating facts if the sale, for any reason, can't be completed.

The other project for this period is for seller and buyer to discuss a training schedule and perhaps plan a campaign that will go into effect after the close, announcing to customers about the new ownership. This may involve a mailing to everyone on the customer list. Perhaps it will make sense for the two of you to visit key clients to let them know the news and to make the introductions. By planning this out now, you'll be ready to implement the program when the time is right.

Sellers, please note that this is the point in the selling process when you will be glad you did the hard work to prepare your company for the transfer. The last few items needed by the lender for final okay on the funding to close escrow, are probably at your finger tips by now. The meetings with the landlord and with key vendors will have paid off as they are aware of what's happening, and what must be done so escrow can honor their claims and requirements. Any problems that occurred were probably handled quickly and efficiently with escrow, because you anticipated most everything that might come up at the end, and you planned accordingly.

The Close

On the day scheduled for close, with the wait time fully elapsed and all needed documents and money in place, the escrow service will have a few final important steps to follow to make the transfer official.

The buyer will be asked to bring a certified or cashier's check for the closing amount, which will include the balance of down payment, the buyer's share of fees, any deposits to be collected through escrow, any sales or use tax on personal property purchased from the seller, and the sum of prorated expenses allocated to the buyer.

The rent might be prorated so that the seller is reimbursed for the part of the month for which rent has been paid, but the seller will no longer own the business. And the seller probably will get any lease deposit refunded, as this item is charged to the buyer. Prorations also can apply to rental of equipment, advertising and promotional contracts and other services for which the seller has prepaid. Personal property taxes also might be prorated.

After documents are signed and checks distributed – the one for the seller, for the broker if any, for payments to various Federal and State agencies to close the seller's accounts and to any other entity with a legitimate claim – the escrow service provider will file the documents that need to be publicly recorded. Among them is the list of personal assets that are being pledged to the seller as collateral for the loan made to the buyer. Any other property, including the buyer's real estate – if it is being used to secure the obligation – also will be identified in an appropriate filing.

This is when the final inventory count is presented to escrow so the seller can receive the exact amount of money for this, either as part of, or in addition to the price – depending on the agreement.

Once these tasks are completed, the documents signed and notarized, and question are answered, the escrow holder will send you off to celebrate, so he or she can finish with the paperwork.

What Can Go Wrong

It was pointed out earlier that there can be some surprises when a transaction is close to completion, if all necessary clearances and approvals haven't been obtained beforehand, or if the parties weren't completely upfront and honest when disclosing their information. If the buyer hasn't the ability to close the deal as promised, or if the seller's financial records don't correspond to earlier statements about the business' performance, there are bound to be problems in the due diligence part of the transaction.

For the seller, there can be additional problems and surprises if the important step of qualifying prospective buyers was not properly conducted.

On occasion, and despite careful precautions, sellers can discover they are dealing with a "buyer" who is excited about the business, easy to get along with – perhaps even charming – but somehow can't seem to get it together on the money part of the equation. The buyer may claim to be eager to purchase the business and may express the opinion that the asking price and terms are quite reasonable. This "buyer" can explain the delay in coming up with the down payment as an error at the bank, or the computer malfunction at the brokerage house where the stock was to be sold. The buyer might even talk about the check getting lost in the mail.

Some buyer pretenders can readily be found out. I'm aware of a prospect who produced a banker recommendation on a phony-looking letterhead for a non-existent financial institution. Another submitted a financial statement so poorly prepared that the addition was incorrect. But others are very good at deception and it may take awhile before the "beast is unmasked."

The seller's first line of defense against dishonest buyers is the intuition developed over years of conducting business. Most likely you have a sense that something is amiss when someone is attempting to defraud you. Nearly all successful business people develop this ability. The problem with eager sellers, of course, is that they sometimes ignore that "internal" voice which keeps trying to get their attention to let them know they are being conned. We're so pleased to find a buyer who wants exactly what we're selling, and who is so nice about it, that we forget to conduct the gut check to determine if it feels like the person is for real.

Just as buyers are conditioned to approach each new business offering with some natural skepticism and caution, sellers should regard every buyer, at the first meeting, with a bit of suspicion until he or she proves to be reliable. Make sure to dole out information slowly and carefully in return for the buyer's disclosures.

And it's very important that sellers maintain their file of prospective buyers so that if the "top" candidate seems to be long on conversation but short on cash, the prepared seller will be in a position to get other buyers interested in the offering. Soliciting back up offers should be part of the strategy in the campaign to sell a business. And make certain that all buyers are aware of this. If they want the business, they'll have to be prepared to deal quickly and honestly.

Other Escrow Surprises

Among the most annoying discoveries in the process of selling a business is that there's a claim in escrow from someone the principals have never heard of, or someone who was paid off a long time ago. And then there's the legitimate claim from a lien holder whom the seller may simply have forgotten.

I classify these as annoyances because they're rarely deal killers. Speed bumps in the road to a completed escrow simply confuse the buyer – perhaps causing him or her to entertain second thoughts about the choice to purchase the business.

Rightful claims that somehow did not get handled before the business went on the market should be taken care of now. Small items can usually be dispatched quickly. One seller was sure she'd paid off a vendor who put a claim for about $100 into the escrow. Rather than waste the time and energy trying to dispute the claim, however, she simply agreed to have it paid again out of the proceeds. Then the buyer put another $50 into the deal, wanting to split the expense as a gesture of goodwill toward the seller.

And if the claim involves a lot of money, you can always agree to have the transaction close on time, with the disputed sums held back in escrow until the issue is resolved. Any false claim from a broker or from anyone else who wants to profit from your deal but can't prove a right to do so, will be quickly dismissed. A seller might even have the opportunity to take the claimant to court with a request for damages because the person falsely tried to profit from the deal and wanted to take advantage of the seller at a difficult and vulnerable time.

The priority is to keep your deal moving forward toward the close, and, whether you are the buyer or the seller, to keep communicating with the other party and with the escrow service about how to best handle any claims or other actions that threaten to delay the completion of your deal.

Major Changes after Sale

And suppose the buyer takes over and has problems keeping the business functioning at a profitable level. This might be the result of a buyer who is unable to manage the business, keep customers happy, work with suppliers and provide competent supervision and leadership for employees. Or it could be the consequence of a dramatic change in the market or the composition of the industry.

What's the seller's role in this scenario? Well, there is only so much the seller can do about this. A smart seller will try to provide some assistance, but the business now belongs to the buyer. The problem belongs primarily to the buyer.

The failing business is the seller's problem only to the extent that it represents security for the obligation owed to seller by the buyer, and if the business is the only collateral. And the seller's liability exposure in a legal sense is limited if he or she was careful, during the marketing and sale of the business, to tell the truth, to provide as much information as possible, and to keep track of what happened with notes and copies of documents maintained on file.

There is no guarantee that the buyer will be successful. And no guarantee that if he or she begins to fail, the seller won't be asked to contribute to a "bail-out," either by invitation to participate in retroactive negotiations, or with a lawsuit that claims the seller created, withheld or misrepresented the facts about the business.

If sellers remain aware of the fact that once in an awhile the sale of a small business leads to unfortunate consequences, such as a failing company, they will be reminded to use caution and intelligence at every step of the process. And apply some of the ideas presented in these pages.

It is recommended that sellers make sure to start with a qualified buyer, supply all relevant information, negotiate for the best arrangement that gets you a deal, share with the buyer your view of realistic expectations for the business, offer to help when appropriate, and keep notes and documents that provide a record of your words and actions. These strategies will help keep the seller's loss to a minimum in the event the buyer doesn't achieve the success which the seller enjoyed with the business.

Conclusion

This review of the final processes is meant to give buyers and sellers an overview of the steps that take place once a transaction for sale of a small business is moved into the final stage at the escrow service or attorney's office. There is not much left for the seller to do except make sure escrow has all the documents needed to comply with the law and respond to any claims from private or governmental organizations if added information is required.

Buyers should busy themselves preparing to operate the newly-acquired company.

And both parties should make an effort to talk as little about the transfer as possible. At lease until it is completed. Then you can make the fact known to everyone with whom the business is associated.

KEY POINTS FROM THIS CHAPTER

❖ *Among the responsibilities of the stakeholder to complete a deal on a small business, are to conduct a lien search, assist with the public notice of the transfer, including a notice of transfer of the liquor license – if applicable, receive claims, request releases from taxing authorities, verify approvals from lenders and others whose okay is needed to close, prepare documents such as promissory notes, confer with the parties about claims in the escrow, calculate prorations of rent and other prepaid expenses, and distribute the money and documents at the close.*

❖ *During this waiting period, it's a good idea for the seller to pay attention to running the business efficiently so everything will be in good order at close of escrow. The buyer's job at this point is to prepare for operation of the business and to plan a campaign to get introduced to the new clients.*

❖ *To the extent possible, parties should avoid talking to customers, employees and others about the planned sale. Of course, you can't be sure your secret will be kept when the fact of the sale has been published in a legal notice newspaper, and perhaps announced with a placard on the front window. But still, the less said, the better – at least until the transfer is completed.*

❖ *The landlord for the business may be involved in the escrow if he is due to receive a sum equal to the increase in the lease deposit and/or to a rent hike.*

❖ *In order to close, the escrow holder will need all the funds scheduled to be distributed to the seller and to any other parties or taxing authorities that have to be paid to clear debts and complete the transaction. Also required will be fees for filings and for any unpaid balance of the escrow fee.*

❖ *Prorations will be calculated and distributed by the escrow company, which also is charged with the responsibility of filing any new liens, security agreements and related documents.*

❖ *Sellers sometimes are charmed by an unqualified buyer who is long on conversation; short on cash. One way for a seller to be alerted to the possibility that a buyer has ulterior motives is to pay attention to your instincts about the person. You often can trust the innate ability to "read" people, developed over years of conducting business. Sellers are cautioned not to let your eagerness to sell overcome your good judgment.*

❖ It's important that sellers maintain a file of prospective buyers – even when there's an accepted offer – so that back-up offers can be solicited.

❖ A business well prepared for sale should yield no deal-killing surprises when examined by a buyer during a due diligence evaluation. To minimize the impact of any problems discovered by a buyer, its best if the seller reassures the buyer that minor problems don't cause major business disruptions.

❖ Unanticipated claims that appear in escrow are usually more an annoyance than a deal wrecker. Communicating with the escrow company as to how to deal with the claims is usually the solution. Escrow can set aside money for the large claims to be dealt with later, and the deal can close as scheduled.

❖ It is very important to keep a deal moving forward at any and all stages. Delays and stalls can kill a transaction. Parties are advised to confer with their escrow service if there appear to be problems that threaten to slow down the process.

❖ There is not a lot that a seller can do for a buyer who's running the business poorly or encountering major difficulties unexpected before the deal closed. If the buyer is open to suggestion, perhaps the seller can offer advice.

❖ Sellers are advised to be aware of the worst that can happen in a deal and let that be a reminder to follow the advice offered in these pages, so as to minimize your exposure to financial loss and to charges that you misled the buyer.

❖ It's a good idea for buyers and sellers to maintain a file with notes and documents that can demonstrate what you said and did during the whole process involving the transaction on a small business.

AFTERWORD

Even a glance at the financial pages of your local newspaper, or a quick scan of the business banner – if you prefer to get your news online – reveals that Americans are experiencing an economic upheaval the likes of which has not been seen in three quarters of a century.

Record federal trade and budget deficits, the fiscal crisis in many sectors of local and state governments, and the dramatic changes in employment all are powerful indicators that a new economic model is quickly replacing the one with which we've become familiar and comfortable.

Regardless of your ideas about the causes and the extent of our economic problems, and the correct solutions, you probably recognize the extent to which our financial lives have changed: A secure corporate job? Affordable health care? A stable dollar, providing Americans strong buying power when abroad? Unwavering confidence in our Social Security system?

These and other components of economic life that we've taken for granted are clearly among the ideas we no longer can rely on as we make the decisions that affect the way we provide for ourselves and our families, and the preparations we make for a secure financial future.

What we can regard as a reliable principle is the importance of self sufficiency. And for millions of Americans, this means the ownership of a small business.

Whether that business is a franchise, a food service company, a retail enterprise, a distribution or manufacturing firm, or a service provider, each small business represents an opportunity for us to participate in the American tradition of entrepreneurship. With our businesses, we have the power to take care of our financial needs with our own labor, and to distinguish ourselves in our enterprises with superior planning, unwavering dedication and hard work.

If you are involved in this vital sector of our economy – either as an owner preparing to sell, an eager business operator-to-be who is determining what kind of enterprise in which to engage, or someone working in between those extremes – this book is dedicated to you. And I offer my sincerest hopes that it provides some ideas and a bit of motivation to help you make your unique contribution for your welfare and for the continued well being of our economy.

RESOURCES

USA Businesses for Sale
800-207-7478
www.usabizmart.com/links

United States Chamber of Commerce
U.S. Chamber of Commerce
1615 H Street, NW
Washington, DC 20062-2000
202-659-6000
800-638-6582
www.uschamber.com

United States Small Business Administration
409 Third Street, SW
Washington, DC 20416
800-U-ASK-SBA
www.sba.gov

National Business Association
5151 Beltline Rd. Suite 1150
Dallas, TX 75254
800-456-0440
972-458-0900
www.nationalbusiness.org

SCORE Association
409 3rd Street, SW
6th Floor
Washington, DC 20024
800-634-0245
www.score.org

International Franchise Association
1350 New York Avenue, NW Suite 900
Washington, D.C. 20005-4709
202-628-8000
www.franchise.org

INDEX